Swiss Straw Work

Techniques of a Fashion Industry

by
Veronica Main

Illustrator Gillian Nott

Designed and Produced by **Carey Company**

MAIN COLLINS PUBLISHING

Acknowledgements

The secrets of the Swiss straw industry would have been locked away forever had it not been for the invaluable assistance of the following very special people.

J. Rudolf Isler, Honorary President of the Foundation of the Freiämter Stroh Museum, Wohlen whose extensive knowledge, enthusiasm, kindness, friendship and generosity made this enormous project possible. Gillian Nott, Illustrator, who worked with great skill for many months, painstakingly recreating in her diagrams every twist and turn of each technique.

In Switzerland

The Board of Directors of the Freiämter Stroh Museum for their support and permission to reproduce some of the photographs used in this book. The Board of Directors of the Schweizerische Stiftung Strohverarbeitung, Freiburg for their support. Brigitte Koch-Berger, whose generosity in sharing her extensive knowledge first inspired straw workers around the world. Ursula Späni-Küng and Rita Boschung-Bielmann, who both shared information and skills. Elisabeth Spinnler-Furrer, who enabled the first contacts between the English and Swiss straw workers. Bethli Rohr-Hunziker, whose work to teach and document techniques provided the first written information. Monika Brügger, whose working knowledge of the industry, in particular the spinning of straw into Schnürli, inspired me. To all my other friends in Switzerland who have provided much valued help and support throughout the years.

In England

The Trustees of the Queen Elizabeth Scholarship. Margaret Bradbury and Peter Shelley, who following their visit to Switzerland in 1986 so willingly shared their knowledge of this industry so that others might learn and enjoy. Debbie McManus, Andrew Nott and Elizabeth Adey who assisted with proof-reading during the book's early stages. Marian Nichols, who throughout has offered valuable advice, support and friendship, whilst guiding me with a steady hand. Kate Richenburg, for her professional advice, which encouraged me to continue when giving up seemed the best option. Gilly Riley, who did the final proof-reading. Jean Macqueen, who compiled the index. Gordon Thwaites, whose considerable engineering skills, patience and interest in the subject recreated the original Swiss tools so that workers can perpetuate the skills of previous generations. Kathryn Main, my hand model. Paul and Jacqui Carey, who have been the consummate professionals, unerringly patient and without whom the book would not have been produced. Finally, but definitely not least, to Peter Main, my ever-patient husband, who is my rock.

Dedicated to my mother

Printed by Brightsea Press.
Designed and produced by Carey Company.
Published by Main Collins Publishing.

ISBN 0-9541795-0-1

CONTENTS

FOREWORD

I am happy and proud to write this foreword: happy that Veronica Main's tenacity and enthusiasm for her subject has resulted in this fine handbook and proud that I have been able to assist her in recording the history of the Swiss Straw Industry started by my forefathers over two hundred years ago.

In 1987 I welcomed a group of British corn dolly makers to our Freiämter Strohmuseum, and although, at the time, I was ignorant of the handicraft they practised, I was intrigued by their knowledgeable enthusiasm for the items on exhibit. This visit was the beginning of friendships with a number of them, and led to mine with the author of this remarkable publication on straw techniques.

Veronica has undertaken the complicated task of analysing and recording the various materials and methods used in creating the most important straw braids and ornaments produced in this region of Switzerland in the 18th and 19th century. By diligent study of actual samples and models of old hats, she has been able to pinpoint the processes and materials used. This, along with her delight in the finished designs, have come together to make this manual as instructive as it is beautiful. I have followed her painstaking research which is the basis for these easily understandable and reliable instructions, printed here for those who wish to duplicate them. I too have profited from her passion for the craft: her knowledge and curiosity have helped me to discover the intricacies of the products my ancestors created and increased my appreciation for their beauty.

The directors of the Freiämter Strohmuseum in Wohlen and the Schweizerische Stiftung für Strohverarbeitung in Freiburg, agreed with me to support this publication, and we are very pleased it will be translated into German, thereby expanding its readership.

Veronica's book ensures that in the years to come, this unique handicraft will be given the attention and recognition it deserves. Even more important is that those who admire it, will be able, with her guidance, to copy established patterns and create their own, using the most humble of raw materials, straw.

Stiftung Freiämter Strohmuseum
J. Rudolf Isler
Honorary President

INTRODUCTION

I am often asked why I have such a passion for investigating the straw work techniques of past centuries. My answer is quite simple: the versatility of straw and the ability of skilled workers to transform stiff stems of straw into strong, flexible materials fascinates me. Precious metal embroidery threads tarnish with age. Fine silks rot, but straw survives more beautifully than any other material.

History seldom credits the workers who were the lifeblood of the straw hat industry. In Switzerland, tens of thousands of men, women and children worked incredibly hard, often for very little reward, to make vast quantities of exquisite items that were destined to decorate hats of the rich and famous around the world. Johann Pestalozzi, the Swiss educational reformer, believed that it was more important to develop capabilities than simply to acquire knowledge. He died in 1827 just as the Swiss straw industry was developing. Surely, had he lived longer he would have been proud to see how when put into practice, his theory created such long-term success for the Swiss people. It was a success that took fashion by storm and left other European hat material manufacturers trailing in the wake of Swiss dominance.

The Freiämter Stroh Museum in Wohlen has an extraordinarily comprehensive display and archive. The techniques described in this book, many of them new to today's workers have been re-discovered during many happy, although sometimes frustrating, hours of research at the museum. I have attempted to recreate faithfully each technique according to samples in the collection. However, I am aware that workers sometimes adapted and changed methods and it has been impossible to include all of these variants. Throughout the book I have used the names for motifs and techniques as they are recorded in the museum collection and documents. When they are unknown a simple descriptive name is provided.

I must acknowledge the invaluable assistance of Mr J Rudolf Isler who shared with me his extensive knowledge. This information is all the more important as he is one of the last people with direct links to the Swiss straw industry. Additionally, many straw workers in Switzerland entrusted me with valued information and I thank them for their generosity.

The book is divided into four working sections. Each one starts with the easiest and ends with the most complex technique. By working through in sequence you will gradually increase your knowledge and easily absorb each new skill.

It is important to realise that originally many of these techniques were taken from various textile industries and adapted for use with straw. Combine this fact with the Swiss workers practice of mixing materials and you have exciting possibilities for development. So in the spirit of the workers, use straw, use textile fibres, mix textile fibres with straw. Be creative and adventurous, but most of all, enjoy!

Veronica Main
April 2003

The straw industry of the Freiamt, 1830.

*D*uring the winter months, when night fell in the Freiamt and its surroundings, whole families, including children and grandparents, would gather around a table in poor light and would sit, sometimes far into the night, making straw plaits and hats, as well as a variety of other straw and horsehair products. Life for them was often miserable, their livelihood was meagre, but these people persevered against the odds. They knew how to adapt to the fickle nature of fashion and to the crises of sales; with endurance they surpassed their artistic achievements again and again. Through creative and patient work, they attained a mastery of the art of straw manufacturing which has yet to find its equal.

Translated and abridged from *Die Technik in der Freiämter, Seetaler und Obwaldner Strohflechterei. (The Techniques of the Freiämter, Seetaler and Obwaldner Straw Industry)* by G. Rodel, 1949. Privately published.

INTRODUCTION

The Italian straw industry is renowned for its Leghorn hats. The importance of the English straw hat industry is widely acknowledged around the world. However, the Swiss straw industry, perhaps the greatest of them all, has never received the recognition it deserves. This is particularly surprising because throughout the 19th century and first half of the 20th century, 98% of all Swiss straw production was exported to the rest of Europe and to the U.S.A. Creativity and fashion-sense made Swiss manufacturers the market leaders, and their products were frequently copied by their European counterparts, notably the Italians. British trade journals of the late 19th century waxed lyrical about the Swiss materials and adornments made for fashionable hats and bonnets. But despite the quality and ubiquity of Swiss straw products, they have been over-looked by subsequent generations. Indeed, museums in many countries have collections showing the very best of Swiss skills but their Swiss provenance is rarely mentioned.

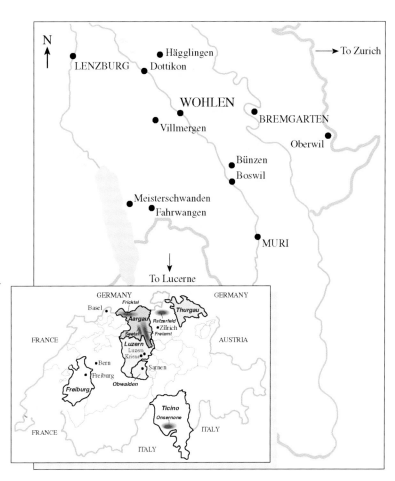

THE FLEDGLING INDUSTRY

In the late 16th century and early 17th century there was widespread development of the European straw plaiting industries, and it is during this period that those of Italy, England and Belgium were first recorded. Early in the 17th century straw plaiting came to the Freiamt, a region of what later became the canton of Aargau. Some scholars have suggested that Swiss mercenaries, returning from Italy, brought home wives who were skilled in the making of straw plaits, and it was they who introduced the craft into the area. However, it should also be noted that in this period farmers needed additional income to pay the high taxes levied by landowners and other authorities.

It seems likely that a combination of circumstances influenced the decision to plait straw, and to make hats. Fortuitously, rye, the straw they first plaited, was cultivated as a crop; the raw material to launch the straw plaiting industry was on hand. Moreover, straw plaiting fitted well in the farming calendar being mainly carried out in the winter months when the land could not be worked.

The importance of straw products in the economic and social structure of the area is first demonstrated in the ledger entries (1643/44) of a regional monastery. They show that tithes were sometimes paid in the form of Schinhüte made by farming families. This practice was to increase, and in the second half of the 17th century was possibly even encouraged by the monasteries. A Schinhut is a large-brimmed, low-crowned hat, painted with a sulphur paste that has the effect of stiffening the straw, thus making it more hard-wearing. These hats were worn locally by women farm workers to protect themselves against the sun. Today they continue to be part of the regional costume.

Gradually, a trade developed; peddlers, travelling from farm to farm selling household items, haberdashery and cloth, often accepted newly made hats as payment. They traded them on to Schinhüetler (hat-peddlers) who distributed them further and further afield until they reached Zurich, Basle and eventually as far as towns in southern Germany.

In 1660 there was, in effect, a trade war. The Guild of Zurich Hatmakers sought to forbid the sale of hats by peddlers who did not live in the town. Not until the Governor of the Freiamt pleaded with the council of Zurich, *in the name of his dear subjects from Hegglingen and Dottikon to reinstate free trade, as it had always been*, was the restriction lifted. Afterwards small family businesses, making and trading straw plait and hats, multiplied, so that by the middle of the 18th century, the straw trade had become increasingly profitable and had replaced the earlier local industries of cotton and silk spinning. Wohlen, which had been a small farming

Hat Peddler
From an illustration by David Herrliberger, 1748.

village in the Freiamt, was to become the centre of a major Swiss industry.

WOHLEN: THE TRADING CENTRE

By 1786 the production and sale of straw plait was more organised, with traders, some of whom had previously been peddlers selling household items, having their own outworkers and trading routes. In January of that year, eight of the major straw plait traders in Wohlen formed an association, which went under the name of Isler & Vock. The document of their agreement is lengthy but makes interesting reading, providing an insight into their life and times. It begins: *In the name of the Holiest Trinity, we, the eight plait traders from Wohlen, namely Small Peter Isler and son Jacob Isler, Andreas Isler with brother Peter, Franz Isler, Jacob Vock, Uolle Wohler and Andreas Dubler have agreed and pledge that we will trade with plait, straw hats, thread, woollen and linen cloth. We will*

respect each other, be honest and hardworking for the benefit of the company... . Twenty-two articles in the agreement covered all eventualities, including remedial action in the event of quarrels between partners, fines if they were found gambling, and a provision for their expulsion if too much time was spent in public houses. It also listed the territory they planned to trade in, namely the Confederation of Switzerland, the Black Forest and Swabia.

In its original form the association of Isler & Vock lasted only one year, but it continued to evolve throughout many changes as partners left to start their own firms. One of the signatories to this agreement, Small Peter's son, Jacob (Jacques) Isler, 1758–1837, was to become a leading pioneer of the future Swiss straw industry, earning a reputation as a resourceful and determined trader and highly respected citizen of Wohlen. Over the years Jacob Isler was joined by his sons and eventually in 1815 the name Jacob Isler & Co. was adopted; a name that was to survive until the late 20th century.

Bonnet decoration of straw plait and pearls.

Of course these developments were happening against a backdrop of turmoil in Europe. Napoleon's troops invaded Switzerland in 1798, bringing a period of upheaval and hardship. Trade suffered badly, until the eventual lifting of travel and trade restrictions gave Wohlen traders the opportunity to expand and continue to provide employment for outworkers. Jacob's sons travelled further afield and successfully established markets in England, France, especially Lyon and Paris,

Holland, Austria, Germany, in what is now the Czech Republic, Prague and even in far distant Russia, St Petersburg.

Napoleon's blockade of England in 1806 gave Switzerland's traders a significant advantage over one of their major competitors, and many new markets were secured at the expense of English dealers. Several years of plenty lay ahead. The year 1809, when business flourished as never before, was remembered into the 20th century in a saying that described a successful year as, *s'gohd wie anne nüni,* (it's going as in the year 1809).

During the first quarter of the 19th century Wohlen straw traders formed new, often short-lived companies and partnerships. From the partnership of Isler & Wohler in 1812, evolved M. Bruggisser & Co. This company was to develop into another of the most important market leaders, manufacturing and selling its products around the world until the second half of the 20th century.

Straw plaiting was conducted as a cottage industry, the makers either selling their products directly to the companies or through dealers. As demand grew, and the number of companies in Wohlen increased, traders began to buy from workers and dealers in other Swiss regions. The most important areas were in the canton of Freiburg, towards the French border, but supplies came also from Rafzer Feld, close to Germany in the northern part of the canton of Zurich, and from Onsernone by the Italian border in the canton of Ticino. In some villages, straw-work schools for children were established, frequently by the local priests who recognised the economic potential of this growing industry.

A REVOLUTION IN PLAITING

The French Revolution affected social structures and fashions in all parts of Europe. For the emerging middle class, straw bonnets became increasingly fashionable. This had a positive effect on the plait-producing areas of Europe, and gave impetus to a number of developments.

So far, only rye straw has been mentioned as a material, but it should be appreciated that from the 18th century, and possibly before, straw hats were also made from a variety of other materials. Wheat straw was used extensively in other European plaiting centres. Italian plaiters used oats and grasses as well as wheat. Palm and wood chip, later called bast, were also widely used throughout Europe. Towards the end of the 19th century and still today, within the straw hat industry, the term straw encompasses a wide range of materials, many having no relationship to any cereal plant.

Rye does not in general make good straw plait as it neither bleaches or dyes well, and so the staple product of the Swiss industry was of lower quality and yet more expensive than English and Italian wheat straw plaits. Some high-quality wheat straw plait was made in the canton of Freiburg, but as demand for the product increased, supplies of wheat plaiting straw were imported from England and Italy. Despite these efforts and the high quality of the plait, prices were still not competitive.

Split straw plaits had been made during the 18th century, but the whole straw stem had to be cut into splints using a knife. This was an unreliable and laborious process. At the end of the 18th century, or perhaps at the beginning of the 19th century, the straw splitter was invented. It was both quick and efficient, and its use spread rapidly, revolutionising the industry.

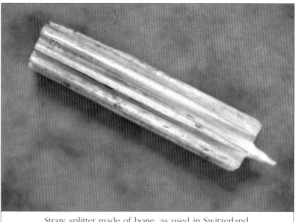

Straw splitter made of bone, as used in Switzerland.

Fortunately, rye straw splits well, producing strong, long splints. In the early part of the 19th century Swiss plaiters used rye splints to make types of plait that were not made elsewhere in Europe. Glanz Zaggli and Ring are narrow plaits made in a range of patterns, from 2mm to 5mm wide; they were used for trimming finished bonnets.

Straw Patent. This fabric was made into bonnets.

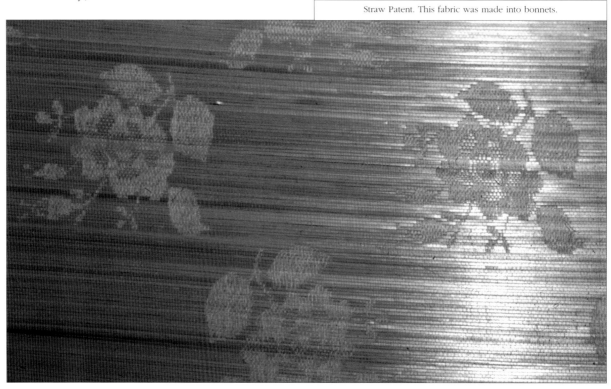

In the first half of the 19th century, whilst plaiters in other European centres contented themselves with creating new plait patterns, the Swiss, thanks to their innate sense of innovation, took an unassailable trading advantage by producing an enormous variety of novel products, often from new materials. It was these, rather than plaits, that were to forge the path to success.

NEW PRODUCTS FROM OLD LOOMS

Weaving had been an important local industry in earlier years and during the 1820s the old looms were taken out of storage and used to weave a fabric known locally as Patent. There were two main types of Patent; both had a warp of silk or cotton. Hemp Patent had a weft of Manila hemp, a material first imported into Switzerland from the Philippines in 1825, whilst the weft of Straw Patent was straw splints. Whereas hemp could be woven with shuttles, straw splints had to be introduced by hand, one by one.

Both types of Patent were durable, light-weight fabrics and surprisingly, in the case of Straw Patent, remarkably flexible. To make fashionable "bonnet merveilleux" the fabric was cut into pattern pieces and then stitched together just as one would use almost any other textile. One very fine and rare example of a Straw Patent bonnet is in the Freiämter Stroh Museum in Wohlen and another in the Boston Museum of Fine Arts, U.S.A.

Sheets of Hemp Patent were turned into another important product. The cloth was stiffened with gelatine, then allowed to dry, after which it was cut into narrow strips from 3mm to 10mm wide. These strips were incorporated into other products or hand-plaited, either alone or with straw.

Placid Isler was possibly the most innovative of Jacob Isler's eight sons. He was a friend of Joseph-Marie Jacquard of Lyon and, in 1825, brought the first Jacquard ribbon-looms to Wohlen where they were adjusted to produce what were known as Bordüren, and in French as Bordures. Bordüren were decorative bands ranging in width from approximately 20mm to 70mm and occasionally wider. As with Patent, they usually had a silk or cotton warp, but the materials used as the weft could be straw, whole or splints, hemp, horsehair, or Schnürli, fine two-ply straw threads, in any combination or on their own. Bordüren were stitched either together, or on to fabric-covered wire frames to produce airy, lightweight bonnets for summer-wear.

Schnürli and split straw Bordüre.

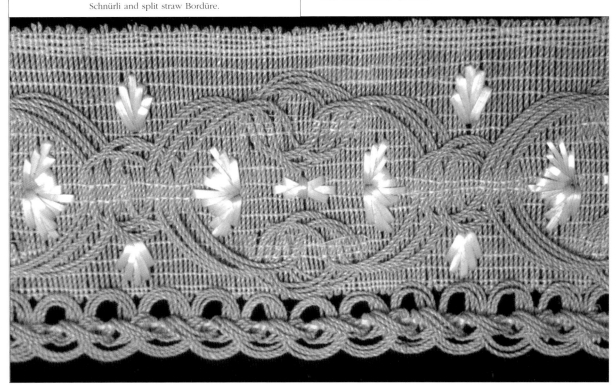

Eventually 16,000 such looms were set up in the homes of workers and were often kept running day and night when demand was high. Demand for Bordüren was so great that production spread to Italian villages, principally Signa, near Florence in Tuscany.

SPINNING STRAW

The spinning wheel for straw, known as the Strohschnürlirädli, in the Aargau, but in the canton of Freiburg called the Strohdrähtlirädli, is mentioned in the 1840s. Its invention is accredited to a family called Abt, who lived in the village of Bünzen. This small and simple hand-operated tabletop machine, ideal for use in this cottage industry, was to bring the most important development in the industry. Its product, a fine two-ply straw thread was made into a myriad of decorations and incorporated into almost every item produced during the 19th and 20th centuries.

Two softened straw splints are attached to two spindles that are in turn connected by a drive belt to the wheel. As the wheel is turned the splints twist on themselves. In the next stage of the process they are plied together into a fine two-ply thread. This thread is known as Schnürli, little strings, in the Aargau and Drähtli, little wires, in the canton of Freiburg. Unfortunately a Schnürli can only be as long as the splints used in its making; most were about 40cm long. It is said that two men could spin 1000 Schnürli in a day's work, one in less than thirty seconds. Over the years many people attempted to find a method of making longer lengths of Schnürli by splicing, but none were successful. Instead the Schnürli had to be hand-knotted together. Surviving knotted lengths are approximately 14 metres long.

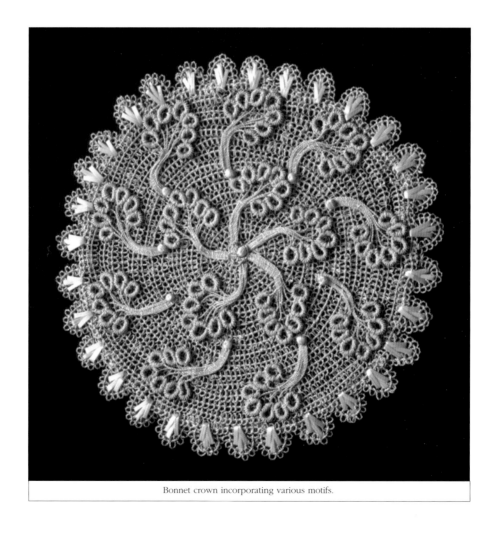
Bonnet crown incorporating various motifs.

This stole was presented to the churches at Boswil and Bünzen.
The Freiämter Stroh Museum has an exhibit of church vestments embroidered during the 1850s by nuns and workers in Wohlen and surrounding villages. The straw imitates gold thread. A variety of straw and horsehair motifs are worked on to velvet. Similar straw embroideries can be found in Bulle and in the Jura region of neighbouring France.

Schnürli were usually left as a natural colour, but fashion sometimes dictated that they should be dyed. Sample books of the 1850s and 1860s at the Freiämter Stroh Museum in Wohlen include Schnürli, made from both straw and Manila hemp, which have been dyed brown, black, purple or green, and Schnürli where natural-coloured and dyed Manila hemp have been spun together to produce a barley-twist effect. To supply the enormous demand during the 19th century, the making of Schnürli spread to Lindenberg and the Black Forest, both areas in Germany, and to various villages in Italy. By the end of the century, English hat trade journals criticised Italian Schnürli as being thick, unevenly plied and less attractive than those from Switzerland and Germany.

Meanwhile with the expansion of trade, mainly with the U.S.A, and the development of new products, the burgeoning straw industry spread beyond the Freiamt into the neighbouring region of the Seetal and to the cantons of Luzern and Obwalden.

HORSEHAIR CHANGES THE INDUSTRY

Around 1830, horsehair was introduced into the straw industry. Besides its novelty as a new material, horsehair was important as it was lightweight and therefore ideally suited for making summer bonnets. Horsetails were imported from as far away as Russia and Argentina, though much of the supply came

Bonnet crown of both straw and horsehair Schnürli.

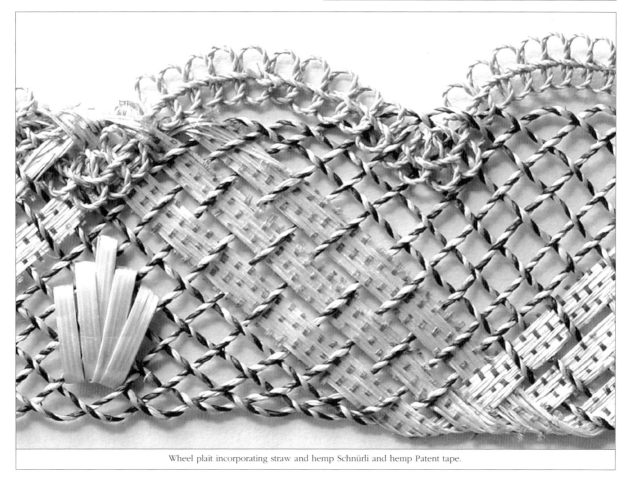

Wheel plait incorporating straw and hemp Schnürli and hemp Patent tape.

from western European countries, principally the region of Galicia in Spain.

The longer the hair, the more expensive it was. Like Manila hemp, it had to be knotted together before being used, but first it needed cleaning and degreasing. A cottage industry of knotting and spooling horsehair flourished, principally in the Entlebuch, canton of Luzern, eventually employing up to 4500 people. A mid-19th century monograph in the Bruggisser & Co. records states that the demand for knotted horsehair was occasionally so great that it had to be weighed out against silver, one matching the other, kilogram for kilogram.

In the late 1840s, Wohlen companies commissioned bobbin-lace makers in the Erzgebirge, on the borders of what is now Germany and the Czech Republic, to manufacture what were known as Blonden. These white horsehair bobbin laces were worked in the same patterns as those used for natural-coloured silk laces. Account books, and the Bruggisser & Co. centenary book of 1912 indicate that Blonden were also made in the cantons of Freiburg and Thurgau, but the Erzgebirge appears to have been the pre-eminent centre. Dark-coloured horsehair, which was usually dyed black, was used to make a fashionable bobbin lace during this period.

The finished laces between 25mm and 100mm wide and 10 metre lengths, or longer, were embroidered with fine straw splints, Schnürli, plaits, beads and other decorations. Horsehair was also spun into Schnürli and used either as an embroidered decoration or as a gimp thread in the bobbin lace. These products were in great demand for the making of bonnets between the early 1840s and mid-1860s and again, but to a lesser extent, in the 1880s.

In Kriens, near Lucerne, a development took place that would have far-reaching consequences for the Freiamt. During the 1840s, a goldsmith and engineer, August Bell, imported French braiding machines for making shoelaces.

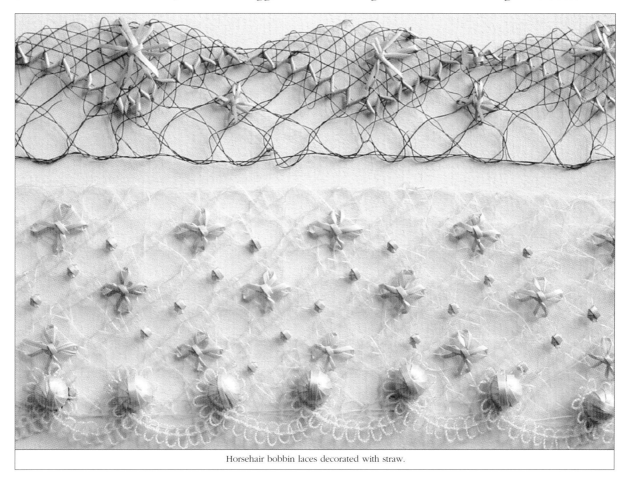

Horsehair bobbin laces decorated with straw.

Next he made tubular braids of knotted horsehair, and then adapted the machines to produce flat braids comparable with straw plait. Whereas straw, due to its short length, was not suited to use on a braiding machine, horsehair because it, like Manila hemp, could be knotted together was, and so Bell's development brought about the beginning of a new era. At first Bell sold his new products to Wohlen merchants, who in turn resold them at very advantageous prices. When Bell found out about this, he cleverly circumvented the Wohlen middlemen by secreting his address in every length of braid delivered, thus enabling direct sales. This forced the hand of the Wohlen merchants who quickly started manufacturing their own machine-made horsehair braids, with the hand-operated machines being set up in the homes of workers. Productivity was boosted by the fact that a single worker, called a Trüller (turner) could operate two machines simultaneously. Soon, factories sprang up first in the Seetal and then in Wohlen, with machines driven by water-power or steam and, later, by electricity. Production soared. In the 1860s, 3,200 machines produced approximately 360 kilograms of horsehair braids per day, and by 1850 the designation Straw industry was replaced by Straw and Horsehair industry, although by 1870 it had reverted once more to Straw industry.

COMPETITION AND CONCERN

All aspects of the straw industry were under constant scrutiny by local and international competitors, and the manufacturers had to fight an ongoing battle to protect their trade secrets. This fear was justified as some industrial espionage actually took place. For instance, as early as 1807, Russians were able to entice a schoolteacher from Dottikon, near Wohlen, who had knowledge of plaiting, to emigrate to St. Petersburg and start a straw-plait business. In the years that followed, other workers went to Russia. By the late 1820s, these migrants to Russia had organised their own industry, thus creating trading difficulties for the Swiss. The rival straw industry in France was also not averse to acquiring knowledge of the industry by any means. In 1828, two Frenchmen from Nancy were caught in the Freiamt trying to recruit workers. They were quickly expelled from the area.

Trading was often unpredictable as other countries such as England, France and Russia, all important customers, would suddenly impose high duties on imports of Swiss straw products in order to protect their own straw industries. The situation became so grave that three of the Wohlen firms, Jacob Isler & Co., Peter Isler & Son and Wohler & Co., presented a petition to the government of the Aargau in 1828.

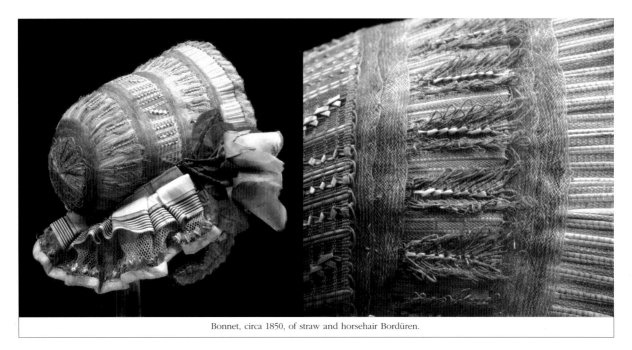

Bonnet, circa 1850, of straw and horsehair Bordüren.

Bonnet ornaments from the period 1860 to 1880 showing ingenious combinations of straw, seashells and beads.

They pleaded for restrictions on the import of straw goods into Switzerland, the export of raw materials, and for the introduction of measures to prevent the emigration of straw workers from the region. Their pleas fell on deaf ears and the government's negative reply is worth recording: *...Your demand for sanctions and the prohibition of emigration is counter to our policy of free trade and violates the freedom of the individual... Solve your problems by working hard, being frugal and maintaining your superiority by being creative...* . This advice seems to have been heeded: ingenuity and skill prevailed to remarkable effect.

CREATIVITY BRINGS PROSPERITY

The ability to create new patterns and novelties made the Swiss straw industry superior to all others. There was careful observation of fashion trends, especially costume, hat and haberdashery embellishments, with popular themes being skilfully adapted to the materials of the straw industry. Innovative products were often devised by the traders or by their ingenious workers. However, it is also known that in 1852, a portrait painter, Johann Anselm Eicher from Muri, was commissioned by Abt & Co. of Bünzen to produce designs, and later he went on to supply them to many other manufacturers. Between 1840 and 1860, there seemed to be no limit to the variety of materials imported into Wohlen: chenille and silk ribbons from Lyon, glass beads from Bohemia and even small iridescent seashells from Venice were all combined with straw and used to decorate new products and fantastic ornaments.

Following the 1862 World Fair in London where French manufactures were exhibiting a glued cotton tape, the Swiss manufacturers realised that its use would be beneficial to their industry. Cotton could be successfully dyed to the latest colours and bleached to perfection; an important advantage since straw and Manila hemp never achieved snow white. A manufacturer in the Seetal, Hegnauer, was able to make a superior product, more soft and supple than the tape from France. Known as cotton lame, it

The knotted hat (Spitzhut, also known as Röhrlihut or chapeaux tuyaux) was worked over a hat block. Long whole bleached straws are knotted together with waxed strong thread. Workers in the canton of Obwalden used the technique to make hats for men, women and children, however during the 20th century, production concentrated on the making of men's boaters. This type of work was introduced at the beginning of the 1800s, but probably did not originate in Switzerland; one theory suggests that the technique arrived from southern Italy.

could be made as almost any desired width, usually about 5mm to 20mm wide. Cotton-threads were glued together, and then flattened between rollers to produce a tape that could easily be plaited by hand or by machine. The tape was manufactured in extremely long lengths, making it ideal for machine production. In the Seetal villages of Fahrwangen and Meisterschwanden, one million skeins of cotton tape measuring 55 metres each were produced annually between 1875 and 1879.

With the flowering of the industry in the 19th century, Wohlen had gone from being a poor farming community to a thriving and wealthy town, with factories and large, gracious homes surrounded by gardens and well-tended fields. The traders travelled extensively, establishing agencies and their own subsidiaries in London, Paris, Florence and New York. The town came to be known throughout Switzerland as Klein Paris (little Paris) and kept this name into the 20th century. It developed a worldly atmosphere thanks to the travelling businessmen imparting the knowledge and use of other languages, bringing back fashionable gifts for their families, as well as, and in quite a few instances, wives from distant countries.

Many of the European straw plaiting centres had focused almost entirely on straw plaits, and found themselves facing insurmountable problems, in the form of new competition from the Orient. Early in the 1870s, the Chinese began exporting straw plaits to Europe, and by the 1890s the Japanese had also established their own significant export market. Hat manufacturers all over the world preferred the low prices that the new suppliers offered. The broad, lightweight Japanese barley-straw plaits were unlike anything seen previously, and quickly became fashionable. The straw plaiters in the canton of Freiburg experienced a severe downturn in demand for their products, but in general the Swiss, having created a great diversity of products, were less dependent on producing plaits and therefore suffered little from this development. Indeed, some Swiss companies enjoyed success by bleaching and dyeing these imported plaits, and then re-exporting them to other hat manufacturing centres.

Bonnet, circa 1880, combining straw and cotton Bordüren.

PIONEERING NEW MATERIALS

During the 1890s, many more new materials were introduced into the industry, a trend that was to increase in the 20th century. Like Manila hemp and cotton before them, these materials could be manufactured into glued tapes, known as lames, which suited both hand and machine production.

One of the most desirable, but expensive, of these was silk lame. There had been several unsuccessful attempts to produce an imitation silk lame. With the first importation of Tussah silk from China in 1890, and in 1895, the development of new machines capable of handling this material it became possible. Silk lames were made into fashionable fancy hand-made or machine-made braids, and so despite the comparatively high price of these products, they were in great demand into the 20th century.

Another new material was ramie, Chinese nettle, which was first used in the late 1890s. Its fibres were short and fine, like those of cotton or linen, and were made into a glued tape up to 10cm wide. It could be dyed and bleached to create new shaded effects, could be cut to almost any width, and was another

tape suited to both hand and machine braiding. Ramie was incorporated into many important products throughout the first half of the 20th century.

In the 1890s other popular materials were, chip, thin wood shavings from willow or poplar trees and bast, a generic term widely used throughout the straw hat industry to include many types of palm and occasionally chip, but at this time used to refer to raffia-like fibres. Mid-decade Cuba bast was introduced; imported from Cuba, this bast was processed by immersion in an acid solution that dissolved the soft tissue leaving only the fibrous structure. Its appearance was lacy and lightweight and, despite its relatively high cost, Cuba bast was in great demand. Additionally, during this decade and into the 20th century, knotted hemp fibres were made into a variety of popular machine-made braids; the best known was Tagal Picot. Unfortunately these braids lacked sheen. When bleached they were never a good white and when dyed black they were never a good black, nonetheless they were the forerunners of a braid which was to bring new sensation to the industry.

Towards the end of the 19th century, the development of viscose, a synthetic material derived from cellulose had a worldwide impact on the textile industry. Now you could produce extruded fibres of infinite length. Known as endless materials these were ideally suited to machine production and therefore reduced the amount of hand labour required.

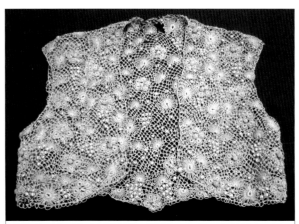
Schnürli transformed into a fabric to create this 20th century bolero.

For Wohlen, it ushered in a completely new phase of manufacturing braids, beginning with crinol (artificial horsehair), visca (artificial straw), Pontova (artificial bast) and rayon (artificial silk), and then other new products including an even more significant material, cellophane.

Invented by Dr Jacques Edwin Brandenberger, a Swiss engineer working in Paris, cellophane became a universally sought-after product for various uses, from packaging to gas masks. In Wohlen, Johann Rudolf Isler (1885–1943) quickly saw its potential. Cellophane was cut into very narrow strips, which were then wound, by machine, around either a single, or multiple knotted hemp fibres to make a fine, round, shiny thread. These threads were made into a machine-made braid called Pedaline, first launched in 1921. Cellophane's shine made this product different from all others, guaranteeing enormous success. Other companies, who imitated Pedaline, gave it their own trade names and later it was also made by competitors in Japan.

The combination of new materials and more sophisticated machines, producing a wide range of intricate patterns and subtle colours brought about an extremely lucrative time for the Swiss straw industry in the 20th century. Its exports were sent around the world, maintaining the industry's importance to fashion.

DECLINE AND RENAISSANCE

With the introduction of synthetics and rise of machine production, in the first half of the 20th century, the use of natural straw declined. Straw plaits and decorations, in fact all forms of straw handwork, were no longer sought after by the doyennes of fashion. The rising cost of manual labour and cheap imports from the Orient meant that home workers increasingly became factory workers. The old-fashioned craft was doomed. Companies made various attempts to revive interest in natural straw, but success was limited to a few expensive, high fashion creations. For example, in 1947, the Paris designer Balenciaga created an outfit of a

New Dawn by Veronica Main, Buckinghamshire, England.

cape and skirt entirely decorated with Schnürli and straw motifs; it was greatly admired but never worn by anyone other than the fashion model.

In 1900, trade directories listed about one hundred manufacturers and traders in and around Wohlen; by 1940 there were only forty. The next three decades saw a gradual ending of this once proud and important industry. The reason was simple: to be chic, or to make a fashion statement a woman no longer wore a hat, hairstyles took the place of hats. In the 1970s, one after another the remaining firms closed. Jacob Isler & Co., the oldest one, was the last to do so in 1991. Now only a small company located in neighbouring Villmergen is still producing machine-made braids. Wohlen has changed. Some of its old factories have been replaced by apartment buildings; others house companies making products suited to the demands of the 21st century.

Fortunately, many stunningly beautiful and exquisitely made products of the Swiss straw industry are preserved in the Freiämter Stroh Museum in Wohlen, and in collections around the world. Craft workers in many countries are recreating the Swiss straw work techniques and in this book I am pleased to be able to present the work of just some of them. Together with this book they and many others will keep alive the history and knowledge for future generations to enjoy.

Knotted hat with Schnürli worked into the knotting by Monika Brügger, Plasselb, Switzerland.

Clockwise from bottom left: Brooch by Atie Nijenhuis-Britting, Ede, The Netherlands.
Corsage by Ursula Späni-Küng, Benzenschwil, Switzerland.
Royal Brooch by Veronica Main, Buckinghamshire, England.

Clockwise from top left: Beaded Spreuer brooch by Linda Meeker, Connecticut, U.S.A.
Thistle by Gillian Nott, Cornwall, England.
Wall Hanging by Liselotte Helfer-Rupp, Bern, Switzerland.

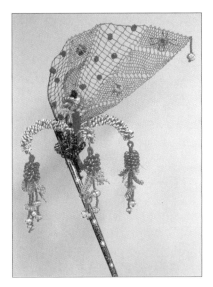

Clockwise from bottom left: Hat decoration or Corsage pin by Janet Christenot, Montana, U.S.A.
Wall hanging by Margaret Bradbury, Herefordshire, England.
Hair decoration by Denise Watts, Surrey, England.
The Cross of Renewal by Marian Vavra, Kansas, U.S.A.
Mary Mary by Peter Shelley, West Midlands, England.
Three-dimensional arrangement by Brigitte Koch-Berger, Bremgarten, Switzerland.

Harmony by Rita Boschung-Bielmann, Rechthalten, Switzerland.

Whilst straw provides an unrivalled beauty, spectacular effects can also be obtained by using other types of thread and fibre. Swiss workers happily used horsehair, bast, wood shavings (chip), hemp, cotton and silk alongside straw. They appreciated the qualities of these materials and were able to select the type best suited to each technique. Do follow their example and be adventurous in your work.

STRAW

Rye is strong and flexible even when split to less than a millimetre wide. Schnürli made from rye are very strong and the characteristic sheen of the straw enhances their appearance. Various split straw motifs, Glanz Zaggli and Ring plaits were traditionally made from rye straw.

Wheat is not as robust as rye; it is lighter both in colour and texture. Schnürli made from some types of wheat straw can lack the sheen of the rye equivalent, and may not be as strong. Plaits made from wheat are more attractive than those made from rye. Wheat straw accepts dye colours better than rye.

Choosing suitable straw

You need a tall-growing variety with a thin-walled hollow stem. Choose straw with stems

Wheat straws, some of the many varieties.

Rye straws.

that are clean, blemish-free and without bends or cracks. Straws with pithy or solid stems are not suitable. The grain head is not used for this work, so is unimportant.

There are many specialist growers offering a range of suitable varieties. Ask their advice as to which straw suits your needs. Some suppliers will send straw by post and just a few will sell prepared straw. Find a supplier by contacting a Straw Work Association in your country, they will offer advice and information. See contact addresses, page 190. Growers normally sell straw by the sheaf, a large bundle of a thousand or more straws. It will have been cut just above the ground so will be long, sometimes over 200cm (72").

Drying

It is important to establish whether or not the sheaf has been dried; damp straw will develop mould and blacken when stored. In good weather the straw can be spread out in the sun to dry and bleach. Raise it above the ground so that air can circulate around. Take the straw in at night, dew will spoil the colour. After about a week, the number of days is dependent upon the weather, the straw will have bleached to a pale cream colour. In bad weather dry the straw in a greenhouse or conservatory, but don't let it get too hot in case it 'bakes' and becomes brittle.

To dry a whole tied sheaf when there is no possibility of spreading it out, loosen the tie holding the sheaf and each day turn the straw at the centre of the sheaf to the outside.

Storing

Choose a place where there is air circulation and normal variable atmospheric conditions; not too damp and not, at the other extreme, constantly dry and hot. In good, vermin and pest free storage conditions straw will keep for many years.

Preparing

Prepared straw takes up less space and can be easily stored in boxes. The top joint length will usually be 36–60cm (14"–24").

Take a straw and look along the length from the head downwards. About 46cm (18") from the base of the head, this distance will vary according to the variety, there is a leaf node. This top section is the most useable part of the plant. Below it there are two or three shorter sections connected by nodes, this straw has been growing for longer and unless bleached with chemicals is usually too brittle. However, sometimes straw from the second section, between the first and second node, can be used to make splints and ribbons.

Cut the straw just above the first node, on the head side of the joint. The leaf will slide off. If it doesn't then you have cut on the lower side of the joint, so cut again. Look at the straw just below the head, there is a ridge at the start of the stem. The head is not required for any project in this book so it can be cut off on the stem side of the ridge.

Grading

Some straws are fine, some are thick; an average sheaf will provide about six different grades, which need to be sorted into separate bundles. To precisely grade small quantities, use a knitting needle gauge to measure each straw. In the 19th century workers, used a series of metal grids to act as sifters for sorting the straw. Once graded, tie the straws into small bundles labelled with the size and type. Put into storage boxes.

Stages of straw preparation.

Bleached and Dyed Straw

In the past, workers bleached the straw before they used it and we should follow their example. The bleaching process improves the colour of straw and makes it softer and therefore easier to work. Bleached straw will take dye colours more readily than natural straw. Dyed straws offer the opportunity to create interesting colour patterns in the motifs and plaits. Instructions for bleaching and dyeing begin on page 181. Ready prepared bleached and dyed straws are available from suppliers in Europe.

Bleached and dyed straws.

GRASS

Harvest tall, hollow-stemmed varieties such as Timothy and Cock's Foot at the flowering stage by cutting the stem just above the root. The stems can be left to dry naturally, in which case they will stay green, or sun bleached, see page 181. Once dry, prepare and store the stems as straw. Use the top and second sections to make plaits and whole straw motifs. Grasses are not normally thick enough to split.

HORSEHAIR

White and brown/black horsehair is imported into Europe from China. Suppliers advertise in textile magazines and on the Internet. Use tail hair; it provides the longest possible length, usually about 75cm (30"). Horsehair can be spun into Schnürli and worked in the same way as straw, or it can be knotted into long lengths for making macramé braids and bobbin lace.

Cleaning

Hair has usually been fumigated and washed before sale, but if you are not sure always clean it before use.

Make a small bunch of hair and tie along its length to prevent tangles. Boil in water with added detergent for 10 to 15 minutes. Drain, and then rinse in warm water, reducing the temperature to a final cold rinse, then dry. Hair can be bleached with hydrogen peroxide. Use the method on page 182.

Grading

The thickness of individual hairs will vary within a bundle, so grade before use.

Bleached and dyed horsehair.

Alternative fibres.

ALTERNATIVE FIBRES

Exciting colourful decorative threads are now widely available. They are easy to use and require no advance preparation, but do be prepared to experiment; some threads are better suited to making certain motifs. In order to accommodate thicker threads it will be necessary to adjust the recommended spacing of needles and template size indicated in the instructions.

Embroidery threads

Lightly glue the cut ends of multi-strand threads to prevent unravelling as you work. Many threads lack the stiffness of straw, and so depending upon their intended use the finished motif may need stiffening with a fabric stiffener.

Waxed-linen thread

Waxed thread does not require additional stiffening. Thicker threads may not be suitable for making some of the smaller motifs.

Viscose tubular braid

Although much larger than Schnürli it can be used to make plaits and decorative edgings. Create three-dimensional work by inserting a fine beading wire into the braid.

String, hemp or sisal

String can be either softer or stiffer than straw, so either choose an appropriate type, or be prepared to apply a fabric stiffener to the finished work.

Paper string

These are stiff enough to hold their shape.

Raffia

Both natural and synthetic raffia can be used, but it may need some stiffening.

Copper and scientific wire

Wire offers many possibilities for functional and 3-D work. It can be incorporated into a Schnürli during its making.

DECORATIONS

Beads and shells

Seed beads can be sewn on to straw sheets. Rocaille beads, sizes 6/0 or 8/0 are normally suitable for threading on to splints, Schnürli and whole straws. For something different add beads to plaits, braids and to some of the motifs.

Embroidery threads, ribbons and chenille

Add to decorative edgings, macramé, wheel plaits and flattened straw ornaments.

OTHER MATERIALS

Paper and card backing for straw sheets

Select a weight of paper or card that is suitable for the project. Also consider whether you need to match the colour of the paper to the straw. Use rice, wheat or mulberry papers, painting, typing/copy papers, or card. When possible choose a paper with a low-acid content.

Fabric backings for straw sheets

Straw can be glued on to a variety of fabrics, ranging from an open-scrim cloth to heavy close-woven cotton. Use scrim, muslin, interfacing materials or buckram. Iron-on interfacing and buckram can be used; follow the manufacturer's instructions regarding temperature.

Glue

Traditionally, animal glues such as fish, rabbit, or hoof and horn were used to fix straw ribbons to a backing. These are still available but fortunately today we can select less messy and highly effective clear, colourless contact glues. Strong PVA glues, such as those used by builders, provide excellent adhesion. Don't use children's PVA glues, they are usually too dilute.

Thread

You need to use thread for securing finished motifs, and for tying groups of motifs together. Choose linen, cotton, or cotton-covered polyester thread of a thickness best suited to the work. Do not use polyester or nylon thread.

Beading or copper wire

The Oberwil techniques incorporate wire into their structure. You need two sizes, 28 and 34 SWG (Standard wire gauge). Wire can also be used to secure groups of motifs.

MEASUREMENTS

The instructions are based on metric measurements. Imperial measurements are usually approximated.

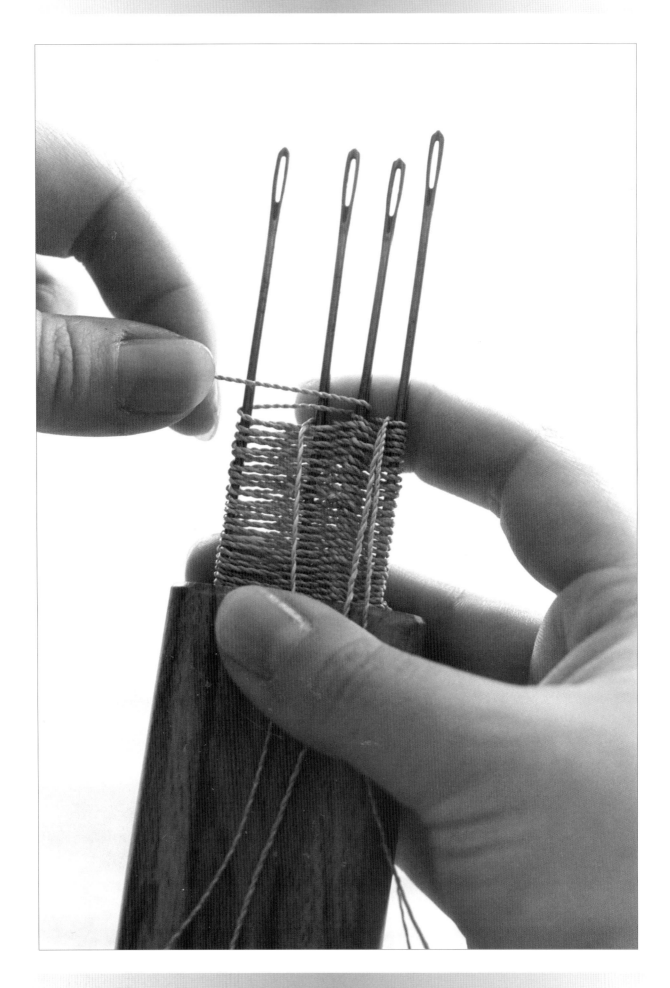

To supply a worldwide demand for their products, workers had to develop an efficient working rhythm and they needed simple effective tools, so that with the minimum of time and effort every motif was a perfect copy of the previous one. Replica Swiss tools can be purchased. Instructions for making your own tools are given on page 186.

GENERAL EQUIPMENT

Embroidery scissors

Straw will blunt the blades so dedicate one pair specifically for straw work. Use curved-blade scissors for the Flattened Straw projects.

Tweezers

These are useful for gripping ends, or for holding motifs during shaping.

Multi-purpose scissors and Wire cutters

Use multi-purpose scissors for straw preparation and general cutting, including thin wire. Use wire cutters for cutting thick wire.

Small bowl and Spray bottle

Use a bowl for holding water to dampen splints and Schnürli, and a spray, filled with water, to dampen the straw whilst working.

Trough or Dish

The dish must be long enough to hold whole straws without bending.

Pin board and Pins

To position damp motifs use long, heavy-duty stainless steel pins with glass bead heads, or use 'T' pins.

Cloth

Always protect the working surfaces.

Basic equipment.

SPLIT STRAW

Splitter

A splitter is a set of cutting fins radiating out from a pointed central spindle. Several types of splitter are available, but all work in the same way. A 6-fin splitter is suitable for most work.

Straw Smoother

The Swiss tool, called a Halmenschaber, is a blunt metal blade set into a wooden handle. A replica, known in England and the United States as "Hindenburg", is shown in the photograph. If you don't want to buy a tool then alternatives are, the edge of a straight-bladed knife, or the smooth edge of a wooden ruler.

Spreuer tool

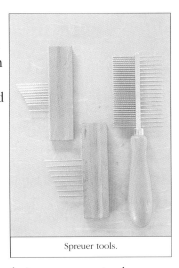

The original tool, a wooden block with pins set along one edge, was designed to produce a specific size of motif. A double-sided, metal-toothed pet comb, with a handle, is an effective alternative, as it allows you to make a wide

Spreuer tools.

variety of shapes and sizes on one tool. Choose a comb with a tine (tooth) rather than a bar at the end. The tines should be spaced about 2mm apart on the fine side and at 5mm on the coarse side.

Before using the comb for the first time mark the spine to correspond with the number of the tine. It avoids repetitive counting when making matching motifs.

Quilling tool

This tool can be purchased through craft outlets. The split pin must hold a 2 to 3mm wide straw.

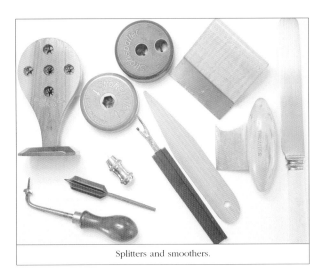

Splitters and smoothers.

Needles

You will need a variety of needles, some are common to all the work, and others are specific. Avoid the use of any needle that has a bulbous eye, as it will make it difficult to remove the finished work. The needle eye must be large enough to take the splint(s).
Darning or **Crewel**, 6cm (2.25") long
Mattress, 20cm (8") long
Candle-maker's wicking, or **bookbinders**, or **short mattress**. The needles need be no longer than 10cm (4") but must not be shorter that 7cm (2.75").

Needle holder

The original tool was a small wooden block that sat comfortably in the hand. Alternatively use a bottle cork or small block of cork, cut to fit into the hand. Remember that the size of motif can be adjusted by increasing or reducing the spacing between the needles.

Needles, holders and quilling tools.

Tensioning block

Traditionally workers used a large heavy log with three nails hammered into the cut end. Instructions for making a small, simple block are given on page 186. Use a table-clamp (G or C clamp) to hold the block in place as you work. The passive wire is wound around the nails to keep it under tension as you work.

Forms

Use a Quilter's bar of suitable width. Or insert either 2 or 3 mattress needles, points downwards, into a cork, side by side, so that they touch along their length.

Wire holder

This is not a necessity but can simplify the manipulation of wire. Adapt an empty film pot as a spool holder, instructions on page 186, or buy a plastic fishing line holder.

Bead centres (forms)

Select forms that are easy to grip such as unvarnished wooden beads. Glass and some plastic beads can be slippery. To make flat beads, use galvanised and plated washers. The form does not need a central hole, unless you intend to sew the finished bead onto a surface, or to link several together.

Sternli tool.

Star tool (Sternli)

The tool has a moveable disc, which when moved downwards reduces the size of the pin circle. This action enables easy removal of the finished motif.

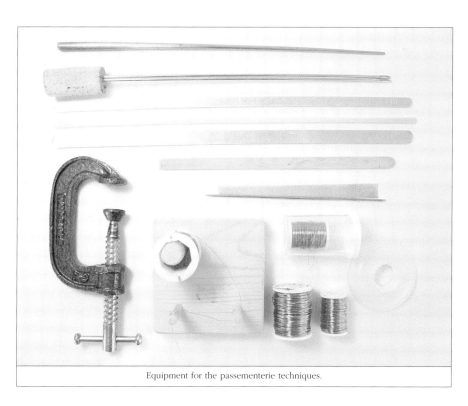

Equipment for the passementerie techniques.

STRAW THREAD

Splitter

As previously described.

Smoother

As previously described.

Straw thread machine (Schnürlirädli or Drähtlirädli)

The function of this machine is to spin straw splints into a two-ply thread. Machines can be purchased. Effective machines can also be built from children's plastic building blocks, or improvised from cord winders or hand drills. Contact a Straw Work Association to find out what their members use.

Needles

To work the full range of techniques you will need to use a variety of needles. Use a long needle, to make large motifs with lots of stitches. Use a short needle, for small motifs with only a few stitches. The thickness of the needle will also affect the finished size of some motifs.

Candle-maker's wicking, or **bookbinders**, or **short mattress**, must be of adequate length to hold the stitches.

Long darning or **crewel**, can be used for making some of the smaller motifs and can be useful for finishing work. They should be not less than 5cm (2") long.

Mattress, or **knitting**, or **cable knitting**, of an appropriate thickness are used in the making of some decorative edgings and macramé. If using knitting needles, remember to remove the end cap.

Needle holder

As previously described.

Straw thread machine.

Square rosette tool

This tool combines needles in a holder, and a zig-zag pattern of headless pins set into wood.

Knotting wheel or Knotting boards

Both of these items can be purchased from Lacemaker's suppliers. The boards are used in pairs.

Wheel Plait wheel (Rädligeflecht-rädli)

This is a wheel around which two rows of headless pins are set in a pattern. The wheel is attached to a stand and clamp, so that it can be fixed to a table edge.

Square rosette tool.

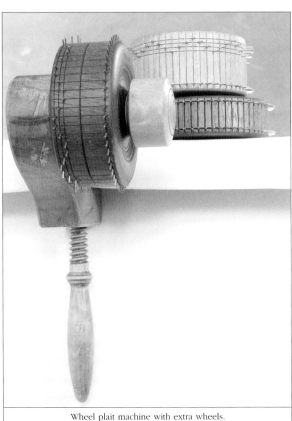
Wheel plait machine with extra wheels.

WHOLE STRAW

Leaf boards

There are a variety of patterns, as shown in the photograph.

Needles

Curved needle, for finishing the leaf motifs
Mattress needle, for making straw pearls.

Forms

As previously described. They are needed when making some of the plaits.

Tensioning block

As previously described. This is used to hold the passive under tension when making some of the plaits.

Leaf boards.

FLATTENED STRAW

Dressmaker's seam ripper

Use this to split a whole straw. Alternative tools are: a long pin, or thin needle, paper clip, scissor blade or a knife.

Smoother

As previously described.

Punches

Use paper punches. Do note that the straw will blunt the cutter more quickly than paper. When using leatherwork punches you will also need a mallet, either rubber or wooden. Hammer on to the cut cross-grain surface of a block of wood, or on to a thick cutting mat.

Craft knife and Cutting board

Use a craft knife with a blade of suitable size for the work, always use a very sharp blade. It's worth investing in a self-healing cutting board, as it will last much longer.

Metal-edge cutting ruler

This is another good investment if you want to work accurately.

Templates, Transfers and Stencils

Buy ready-made craft templates or draw your own shapes. Iron-on transfers can be applied directly to the back of the straw sheet. Use ready-made metal stencils or make your own from thick plastic or from thick firm card.

Embossing tool(s) with ballpoint tip

These are sold in a range of sizes. It may be necessary to use various sizes of ballpoint tip according to the size and intricacy of the motif.

Paper-corrugating tool

The width of rollers will restrict the size of straw sheet or motif that can be fed through.

Plastic and clay craft moulds

There are lots of suitable moulds in craft shops. Choose simple designs and avoid moulds with sharp contours.

Needles

Beading or other types of embroidery needles are required for applying surface decorations.

Tools for Flattened Straw work.

SPLIT STRAW

Preparation:	**Selecting, Splitting, Softening, Storing, Dampening, Before you begin**
Spreuer:	**Basic, Curled, Half, Large without joins, Striped, Large with joins, Banded, Sheaf, Bow**
Quilling:	**Roll, Watch Spring**
Passementerie:	**Rosette, Hop**
Winding:	**Little Star**
Beads:	**Basic, Peardrop**
Figure of Eight with two working ends:	**Shovel, Small Half Moon**

Preparation

Until the introduction of the straw splitter the use of split straw was limited, but following the introduction of this simple, effective tool, workers quickly developed new products. The motifs in this section owe their existence to the adventurous nature of the Swiss who were quick to adapt techniques more normally associated with other materials.

Selecting straw

Both wheat and rye are suitable. For the Fork work and Oberwil techniques, rye straw gives the most attractive results.

Splitting straw

Use the complete, headless, length of the top section, choosing straws that are free from cracks and blemishes.
Straw can be split whilst either damp or dry. Cut the end of the straw so that it is level. Insert the point of the splitter into the end making sure that it is at right angles to the fins. Push the straw over the fins. Once 5cm (2") has been cut continue by pulling the straw. Pull evenly and check that you are pulling at right angles to the fins. The cut straws are called splints.
If you have only one splitter and need to produce narrow splints, split a thin straw. To make wider splints, split a thick straw.

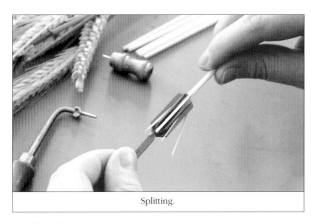
Splitting.

Softening

This process is absolutely essential. The splints must always be thoroughly softened before use. Once prepared the splint curls, feels soft and is flexible even when dry. Using a straw smoother stroke along the pith side, working only in one direction until it starts to curl. The process crushes the pith; it does not remove it. However, a document in the collection of the Freiämter Stroh Museum indicates that occasionally, in order to make

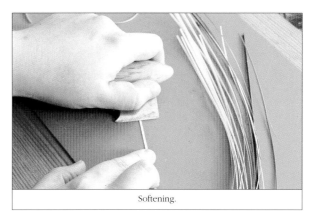
Softening.

rye straw flexible, workers had to remove some pith.

Storing

Loosely tied bundles of dry splints can be stored in a box until required.

Dampening

Unless stated otherwise, the splints must be worked whilst damp. It will be necessary to re-damp the splints during working. Use a spray, or dampen a cloth and wipe it along the splint.
Immerse the splints in warm water, no hotter than hand-hot, until they are pliable, usually one or two minutes. Do not soak for longer, the straw's colour and lustre will be spoilt. Bleached and dyed straws will require a shorter soaking time.

Before you begin

All the instructions are written for use with straw splints. You may need to adjust the spacing between needles and the number of stitches when using other fibres.
For reasons of clarity some diagrams do not show all the repeated working moves.
When you see a diagram where the ends of the needles are dotted it tells you that they are in the holder, but the holder may not be shown.
All imperial measurements are approximated.

Spreuer

The English name for this motif is chaff, but because the original Swiss name is in widespread use the translation has not been used. The Spreuer was one of the industry's most popular motifs, first appearing as a stitched decoration and later as a self-supporting motif. It is a very versatile motif with many pattern possibilities, so once you have learnt the basics begin to experiment.

Basic Spreuer

Begin by using a 2mm wide splint and follow the tine numbers provided in these instructions before you go on to create your own shapes by varying the winding pattern. There are two ways of finishing the Spreuer; I suggest that you become familiar with the first before moving on to the second method.

You will need:

    1 prepared splint 33cm (13")
    Spreuer tool
    Darning needle, optional

Starting ~ basic method

1. Lay the wide end of the damp splint, pith side facing you, behind the tool with a short end (approx. 5mm) between tines 2 and 3, pointing to the front and upwards. *(Fig. 1)*
2. Put a finger behind the tool and hold the splint in place.
3. Fold the splint around tine 1 to the front of the tool. Take the end upwards and then slide it over tine 7. Bring the end down the back of the tool. *(Fig. 2)*
4. Lay it precisely on top of the splint already on tine 1. Pull to tighten and hold in place.

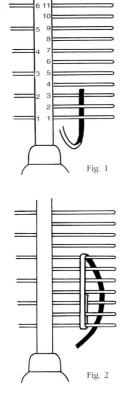

Fig. 1

Fig. 2

Working

1. Fold the end upward over the front of the tool taking it to the left-hand side of the first winding and then fold it over tine 6. Bring the end down the back of the tool. *(Fig. 3)*
2. Pull tight and hold in place on top of the windings on tine 1.
3. Repeat step 1, but this time take the splint to the right-hand side of the first winding.
4. Continue working alternate sides down to tine 4. *(Fig. 4)*
5. Wind the splint with an even tension, neatly stacking the windings as they turn around tine 1. If you do not then the finished motif may spring open when removed from the tool. You must leave 5cm (2") of unused splint for finishing.

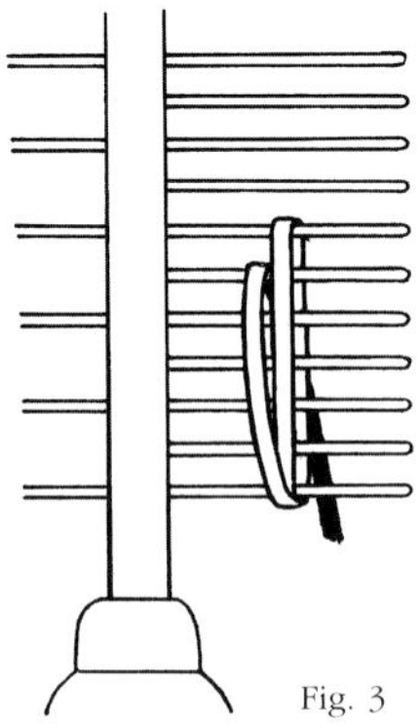

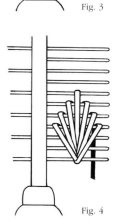

Fig. 3

Fig. 4

Spreuer

Finishing ~ basic method 1

1. Hold the working end under your finger. Turn the tool away from you so that the back of the Spreuer is facing you. *(Fig. 5)*

2. Take the end across the back of the Spreuer to the left-hand side. Thread it through the centre of the windings: through the space between tines 1 and 2. Pull the end, but leave a small loop. *(Fig. 6)*

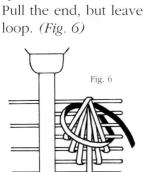

3. If the end will not slide through the gap, either cut the tip to an angle, or use a needle.
4. Pass the end through the loop, from tine 7 towards tine 1. Avoid twisting the splint. *(Fig. 7)*

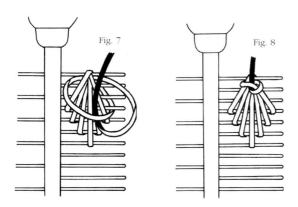

5. Pull the splint to tighten the first loop, then pull to tighten the second. *(Fig. 8)*
6. Keep the knot on the back of the windings, if it is too close to the end the Spreuer will spread open.
7. Gently slide the Spreuer off the tool.

Handy hint
Twisting the splint will cause it to break. If you experience problems this is probably the cause.

Finishing ~ basic method 2

1. Turn the tool away from you and hold the splint against the windings, close to the end of the comb. On the diagram the position is indicated by the bend in the splint. Thread the end between the windings, passing from left to right. Pull, leaving a small loop. *(Fig. 9)*

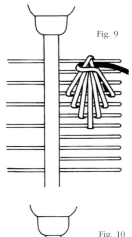

2. Wrap the end completely around the outside of the Spreuer, between tine 1 and tine 2. The end is pointing towards you. *(Fig. 10)*

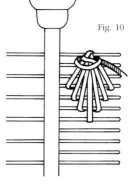

3. Thread the end through the first loop, from tine 7 towards tine 1. *(Fig. 11)*

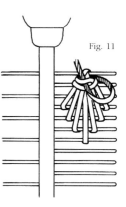

4. Pull on the second loop, at a point where it will tighten the first loop. Then pull the end to tighten the second loop. *(Fig. 12)*
5. Gently slide the Spreuer off the tool.

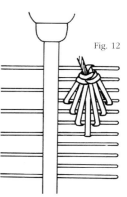

Basic method 2.

Spreuer

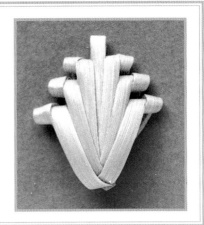

Curled Spreuer

This motif uses more straw so you will need a longer splint, especially if you want to make a larger Spreuer.

You will need:

  1 splint 46cm (18")
  Spreuer tool
  Darning needle, optional

Starting

1. Use the basic method.

Working

1. Fold the end upwards, taking it to the left-hand side of the first winding and then fold it over tine 6, so that the end is at the back.

Thread the end to the front, through the space between tines 5 and 6. Pull tight then thread it to the back, through the space between tines 6 and 7. Bring the end down the back to tine 1. *(Fig. 13)*

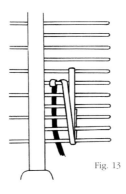

Fig. 13

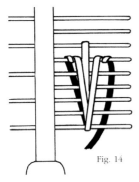

Fig. 14

2. Lay it precisely on top of the splint already on tine 1. Pull to tighten and hold in place.

3. Repeat step 1, this time on the right-hand side of the first winding. *(Fig. 14)*

4. Ensure that the splint sits precisely on top of the first winding on tine 1.

5. Continue working alternate sides down to tine 4. *(Fig. 15)*

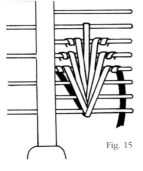

Fig. 15

Finishing

1. Use either of the basic methods.

These are just some of the many possible variations.

Spreuer

Half Spreuer

This can be made plain, with curls, or with both for a really elaborate effect. Use a wider split (3mm) to provide stability as the windings are stacked around tine 1.

You will need:

    1 splint 25cm (10")
    Spreuer tool
    Darning needle, optional

Starting

1. Use the basic method.

Working

1. Wind the splint only on one side. *(Fig. 16)*
2. Have patience; sometimes it can be difficult to control the splint during winding and stacking around tine 1, particularly when making a motif with more windings. With practice it becomes easier.

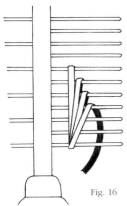

Fig. 16

Finishing

1. Use either of the basic methods.

Variation

The Half Spreuer can be made with the windings to the left or to the right.
Use the winding technique for making the Curled Spreuer.
Once you have mastered the technique make this Spreuer with a combination of plain and curled windings.

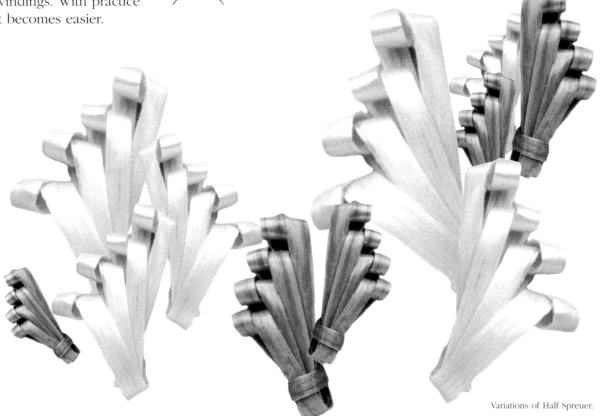

Variations of Half Spreuer.

Spreuer

Large Spreuer without joins

Sometimes you will want to make a large Spreuer but are restricted by the length of splint. The solution is easy, use two splints and effectively double the length. This method also provides colour pattern options, as shown by the shading of one splint in the diagrams. One splint works down the left-hand side of the Spreuer and the other down the right-hand side.

You will need:

>2 splints each 33cm (13")
>Spreuer tool
>Darning needle, optional

Starting

1. Use the basic method with the following variation. Lay one splint on top of the other matching the wide ends, and with both pith sides facing you. *(Fig. 17)*

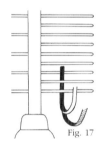

Fig. 17

Working

1. Fold the uppermost splint up to the left-hand side of the first winding. Slide the end over tine 6 then bring it down to tine 1. Tighten and hold in place. *(Fig. 18)*

2. Work the second splint and make a matching winding on the right-hand side. Take care to precisely stack each winding on tine 1. When you change the working splint it can be difficult to hold both in place. Do not worry, it will become easier with practice.

3. Repeat Working steps 1 and 2 down to tine 4, or until 5cm (2") of each splint remains. *(Fig. 19)*

Finishing

1. Use the basic method 1, working both splints as one. You may wish to use a needle to help with the threading. *(Fig. 20)*

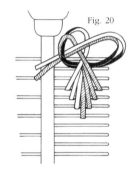

Fig. 20

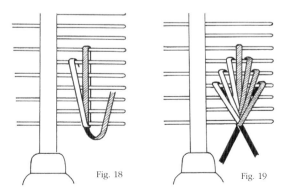

Fig. 18   Fig. 19

A variation of the winding pattern and straw beads create a very different Spreuer.

Spreuer

Striped Spreuer

Now you are familiar with working two splints you can create a striped effect by crossing the splints as they pass around tine 1.

You will need:

> 2 splints of different colours each 33cm (13")
> Spreuer tool
> Darning needle, optional

Starting

1. Use the method for Large Spreuer without joins, but make the following variations. Place the dyed splint on top of the natural one.
2. Wind both splints around tine 7 positioning them side by side, with the dyed splint on the left. Bring both ends down to tine 1, and stack with the dyed splint in front of the natural splint. Hold in place.

Working

1. Fold the dyed end upwards and hold in place on the right-hand side. This keeps the end out of the way whilst the next move is made.

2. Fold the natural splint up to and around tine 6, passing it to the left of the first winding. Bring it down the back and lay it on top of the windings on tine 1.
3. Now wind the dyed splint around tine 6, on the right-hand side. Stack it neatly under the natural splint on tine 1.
4. Continue Working steps 1 to 3. Be aware that in the next, and subsequent alternate working sequences the natural splint is folded upwards in step 1. *(Fig. 21)*

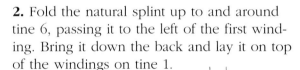
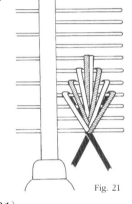

Fig. 21

Finishing

1. Use the method for finishing Large Spreuer without joins.

The Schnürli is added to a finished Spreuer. Starting at the shortest fold and working towards the longest one, wind a Schnürli through the folds. Tie off the ends.

Spreuer

Large Spreuer with joins

This time you work the first splint and then join a second. This technique provides the opportunity to create very pretty patterns. Use this method to make a very large motif, or as a way of joining if a splint breaks.

You will need:

> 2 splints, natural or different colours each 40cm (16")
> Spreuer tool
> Darning needle, optional

Starting

1. Use the basic method with the following variation. Make a curled winding around tine 11, first on the left and then, without bringing the splint down to tine 1, repeat the move on the right-hand side. There is a curl each side of the first winding.
2. Bring the splint down to tine 1 and stack neatly on the first.

Working

1. Using the method for the Curled Spreuer work down to tine 9. There are two curled windings on each side of the first.
2. Finish by using the basic method 1. Trim the end, so that it is level with tine 1.

Joining

1. Insert the second splint, with the pith side upwards, from behind the tool. Pass it from right to left through the centre of the windings, between tines 1 and 2. The short end is on the left. You may need to use a needle. *(Fig. 22)*

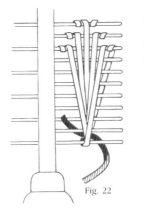

2. Adjust the splint so that it stacks on top of the windings on tine 1. Hold in place.

Fig. 22

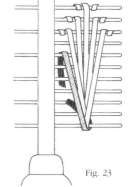

3. Starting on the left-hand side wind around tine 7. *(Fig. 23)*
4. Continue winding, making as many pairs of moves as you want.

Fig. 23

Finishing

1. Use either of the basic methods.
2. Trim off the end of the joined splint.

The Spreuer have been wired to create a flower bough. The background leaves are flattened dyed straw.

Spreuer

Banded Spreuer

Unless you have a very long splint you will have to join a new splint when you make this Spreuer. The joining method is a little different from that used for the Large Spreuer with joins.

You will need:

> 1 splint 50cm (20") or
> 2 lengths of splint 28cm (11")
> Spreuer tool
> Darning needle

Starting

1. Use the basic method, making the first plain winding around tine 11.

Working

1. Wind around tine 9 first on the left, then again on the right of the first winding. *(Fig. 24)*

Fig. 24

2. Bring the end down the back of the tool, to the left-hand space between tines 7 and 8. Thread it through to the front. Gently pull it across to the right-hand side and then pass it to the back between tines 7 and 8. *(Fig. 25)*

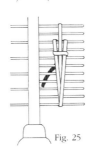
Fig. 25

3. Turn the tool so the back of the work faces you. Using a needle (not shown) thread the end through the loop, towards tine 1. *(Fig. 26)*

Fig. 26

4. Remove the needle and gently tighten the loop. Twist the splint so that the shiny side of the splint faces you. Turn the tool over.

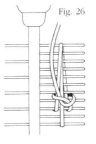

5. Repeat step 1, but make the next two windings around tine 8, first on the left and then on the right. *(Fig. 27)*

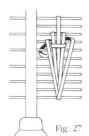
Fig. 27

6. Repeat steps 2 and 3; this time the end passes between tines 6 and 7.

7. Continue working down the tines using the same sequence until not less than 5cm (2") of the splint remains.

Joining

1. Join once the knot in Working step 3 has been made. Trim the old end to 3mm below the knot.

2. Match the width and colour of the old and new splints and using a needle (not shown) thread the new splint, pith side down, under the knot. The short end points towards the top of the tool *(Fig. 28)*. Fold about 5mm of this end down, toward tine 1, and carry on working until the required number of sequences are completed.

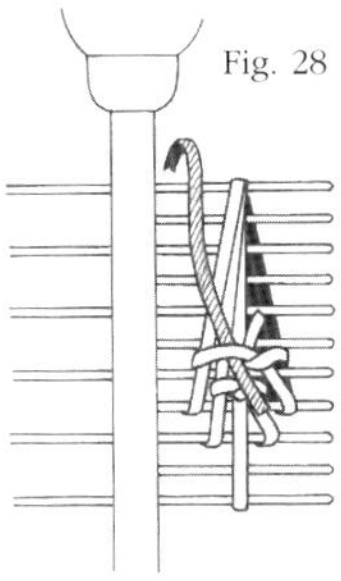

Fig. 28

Finishing

1. End the working sequence at step 3, the knot will secure the Spreuer.

Spreuer

Sheaf Spreuer

To create the flat base of the sheaf the splints are wound side by side along the bottom tine. This Spreuer can be made at the end of the tool as in the previous instructions, or in the centre of the tool, as shown in the diagrams.

You will need:
> 1 splint 46cm (18")
> Spreuer tool
> Darning needle, optional

Starting

1. Use the basic method with the following variation. Wind around tine 10 and then bring the end down to the left of the first winding on tine 1. *(Fig. 29)*

Fig. 29

This tiny angel is made from different types of Spreuer with a straw bead for a head.

Working

1. Take the splint diagonally across the front of the winding to the right-hand side. Make a curl around tine 9. Bring the splint downward to tine 1 so that it lays to the right of the first. Fold the splint to the front.

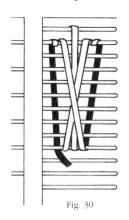

2. Take the splint diagonally across the front to tine 9. Make a curl around the tine. Bring the end down the left-hand side to tine 1. Fold the splint to the front. *(Fig. 30)*

Fig. 30

3. Continue until there are three curled windings each side of the first. Make sure that the splints lay neatly side by side along the bottom tine. *(Fig. 31)*

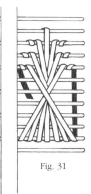

Fig. 31

Finishing

1. Use basic method 2 and make the band around the point where the splints cross on the front.

Spreuer

Bow Spreuer

The start and finish points are in the centre of the Spreuer. This motif can be made at the end or in the centre of the tool.

You will need:

> 1 splint 46cm (18")
> Spreuer tool
> Darning needle, optional

Starting

1. Lay the wide end of the splint, pith side facing you, behind the tool with a short end (approx. 5mm) pointing to the front, and upwards between tines at the centre of the tool. Hold the splint in place.
2. Count down 5 tines and wind the splint around that tine. Pull tight and hold in place.
3. Fold the splint upward over the starting point and then wind around the 5th tine above. Pull downwards, tighten and hold in place.

Working

1. Wind around the 4th tine below the starting point on the left of the first winding. *(Fig. 32)*
2. Fold the splint upward and diagonally across the front of the first winding, then around the right-hand side of the 4th tine above the start.

Fig. 32

3. Bring the splint down the back on the right-hand side, and wind around the 4th tine below the start point. *(Fig. 33)*
4. Take the splint up and diagonally across the front to the left, wind around the 4th tine above the start. Bring the end downwards.

Fig. 33

5. Repeat Working steps 1 to 4 making the last set of windings around the 2nd tines above and below the start. *(Fig. 34)*

Fig. 34

Finishing

1. Use basic method 2 to create the band across the centre of the bow.

To make this cross of Sewn Spreuer, first use a thick needle to make holes, following the shape of the Spreuer, through the backing card. Cut the ends of the prepared splint to a point and follow the basic Spreuer instructions stitching through the card rather than using the tool.

Quilling

Perhaps the 19th century popular revival of paper filigree or paper quilling work first attracted the Swiss workers to these skills. In this section I have only included shapes that I have discovered in the collection of the Freiämter Stroh Museum, but all of today's quilled shapes can be made with splints. The splints must be thoroughly softened and used dry.

Roll

This motif can be worked with any width of splint, but looks impressive when made from a wide splint. Add it to the work with the shiny side of the roll uppermost. Rolls made from narrow splints can be set on their side.

You will need:

>1 dry splint approximately 3mm wide and 15cm (6") long
>Thread, 10cm (4")
>Quilling tool

Starting

1. Put the end of the splint in the quilling tool slot with the pith side facing you.
2. Lay the thread parallel to the needle so that the midpoint rests across the splint at right angles. *(Fig. 35)*

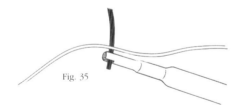

Fig. 35

Working

1. Wind the splint around the tool until 3cm (1") of splint remains. Make sure that the thread does not become tangled in the winding.
2. Hold the splint securely and ease off the tool.

Finishing

1. Fasten by knotting together both ends of the thread.
2. Trim the ends of thread and splint.

Quilling

Watch Spring (Uhrenfedern)

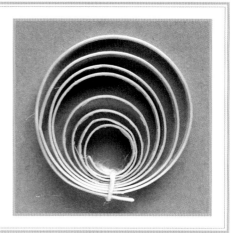

Practice makes perfect with this motif. Once you can establish a working rhythm it can be made very quickly.

You will need:
> 1 dry splint approximately 3mm wide and
> 31cm (12+") long
> Thread, 10cm (4")
> Quilling tool

Starting

1. Put the end of the splint in the needle slot and have the pith side facing you.

Working

1. Roll the splint to 5cm (2") from the end.
2. Hold the end against the last winding.
3. Twist the tool to loosen the roll, from the centre outward. Remove the needle. Control the splint whilst allowing it to unwind.

Finishing

1. Slip the thread through the centre of the motif.
2. Knot both ends of the thread and then trim the ends.
3. If necessary adjust the shape.

Watch Springs decorate this bonnet, circa 1880. They have been sewn on with chenille (detail on opposite page).

Variation

Pinch the tied end of the finished watch spring motif to make a teardrop. The pinched end can be decorated by winding around a Schnürli.

Squeeze the tied end of the Watch Spring.

A Teardrop motif finished with a Schnürli.

> ***Handy hint***
> *The motifs in this section can be made on a Spreuer tool or make a quilling tool by pushing an adapted wicking needle through the centre of a cork.*

Passementerie

Workers in the village of Oberwil produced a range of products known as Oberwiler rolls (rollen), or cord work (Drahtgeflechte). Their technique is taken from conventional passementerie and was used to make individual motifs and long lengths of decoration for use as hat crown or brim decorations.

Rosette (Oberwiler Rösli)

The final winding of the rosette will determine the finished shape, pull it tight and it will be flower-like, leave it loose and it is a rosette.

You will need:

Tensioning block and clamp
Wire 28 SWG and 34 SWG
Form 6mm (0.25") wide and 2mm thick
Splints, 2mm wide
Wire cutters
Wicking needle

Starting

1. Clamp the block to the edge of the working surface. Set up the spool of thicker wire (28 SWG). *(Fig. 36)*

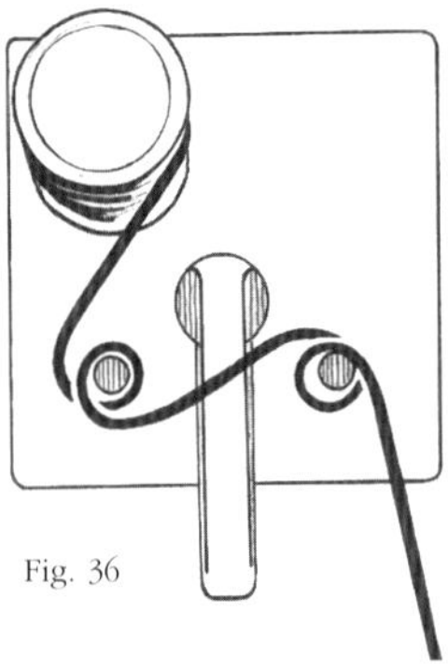

2. Knot together the thick and thin wires leaving 5cm (2") ends. *(Fig. 37)*

3. Hold the form to the left and parallel to the thick wire. When using a wedge shape form the thinnest part is adjacent to the thick wire.

4. Wrap the ends of wire around the lower end of the form.

5. Lay the splint shiny side up, across the form so that the short end of the splint is on the right, and between the two wires. *(Fig. 38)*

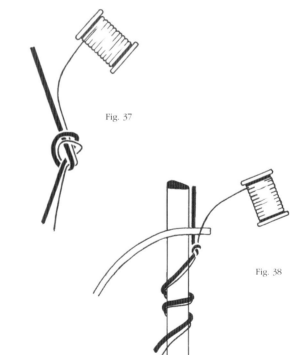

Fig. 36

Fig. 37

Fig. 38

> **Handy hint**
> *Work with dry splints when using a natural wood form.*

Passementerie

Working

1. Tilt the form to the left creating an angle with the wire. Take the thin wire and drop it down between the thick wire and the form. Gently pull downwards so that it fastens the splint to the wires, tight enough to grip, but not tight enough to cut the splint. *(Fig. 39)*

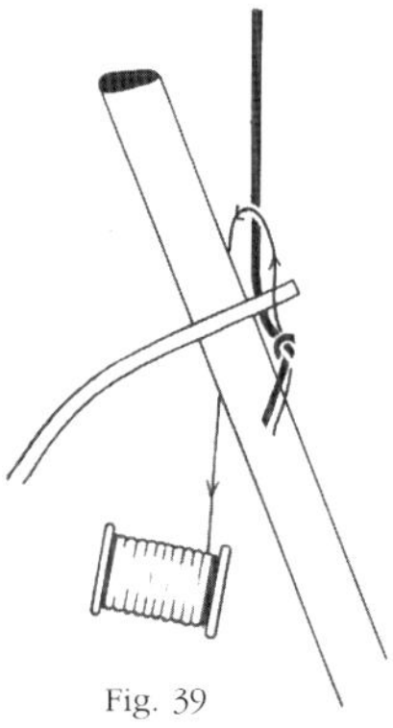

Fig. 39

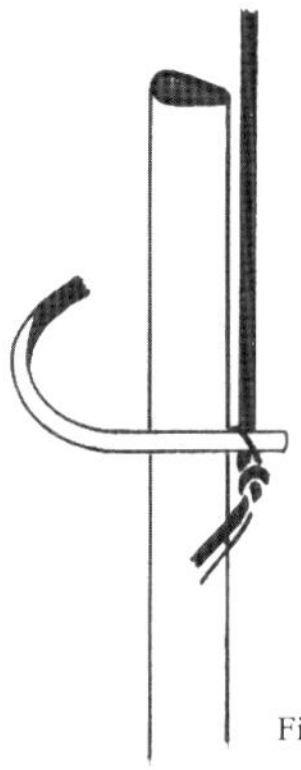

Fig. 40

2. Move the form so that it is parallel to, and touching the thick wire. *(Fig. 40)*

3. Wind the splint once around the form and thick wire. Do not wrap the splint too tightly. The long end is pointing to the left. *(Fig. 41)*

4. Repeat Working steps 1 to 3 until you have a 5–7.5cm (2–3") length. It will be necessary to join new splints.

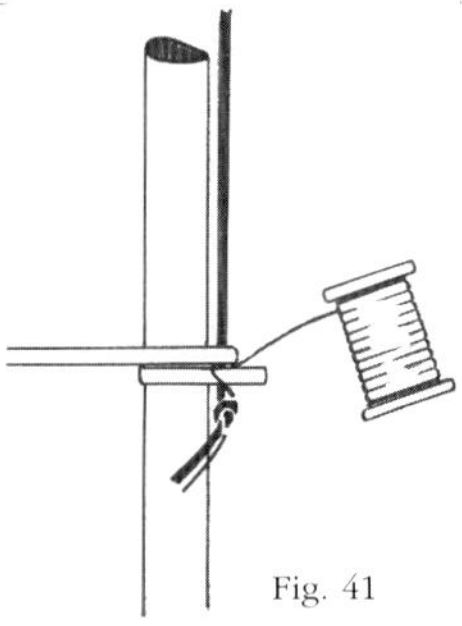

Fig. 41

> ***Handy hint***
> *Develop the tilting movements into a regular rhythm to produce even winding.*

Joining

1. Wind the old end so that it is underneath the form and thick wire, and pointing to the right. The new splint must match the width and colour of the old.

2. Put the new splint, short end to the left behind the old end. *(Fig. 42)*

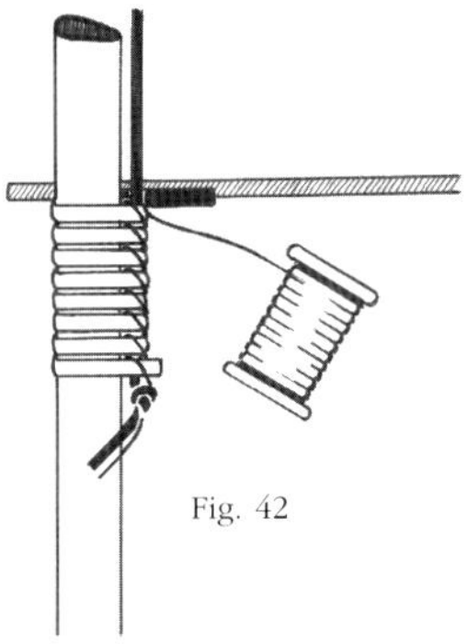

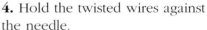

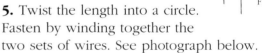

Fig. 42

3. Wrap both ends over the front of the form so that both point to the left. *(Fig. 43)*

4. Make the fastening move, Working step 1. The old end will be trimmed during finishing.

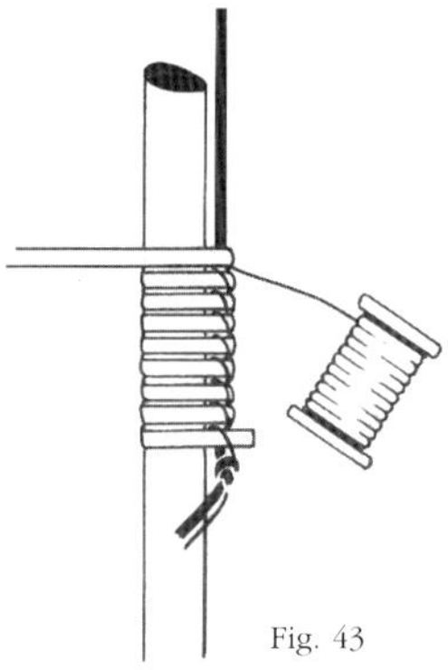

Fig. 43

Finishing

1. Wind the thick and thin wires together to make a 2cm (1") length. *(Fig. 44)*

2. Cut the wires.

3. Trim the splint ends not less than 6mm (0.25") from the wires. The ends can be trimmed shorter once the rosette is finished, but if you trim them too short now they may slide out from the between the wires. Slide the work off the form.

4. Hold the twisted wires against the needle.

5. Twist the length into a circle. Fasten by winding together the two sets of wires. See photograph below.

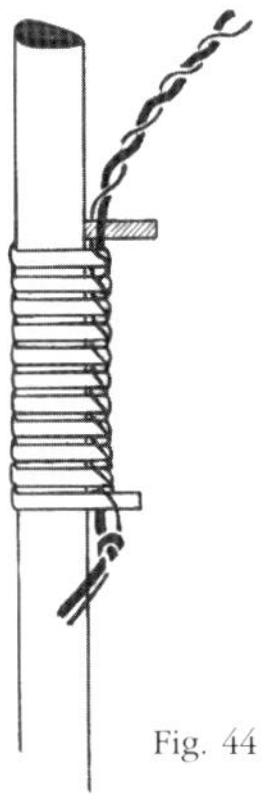

Fig. 44

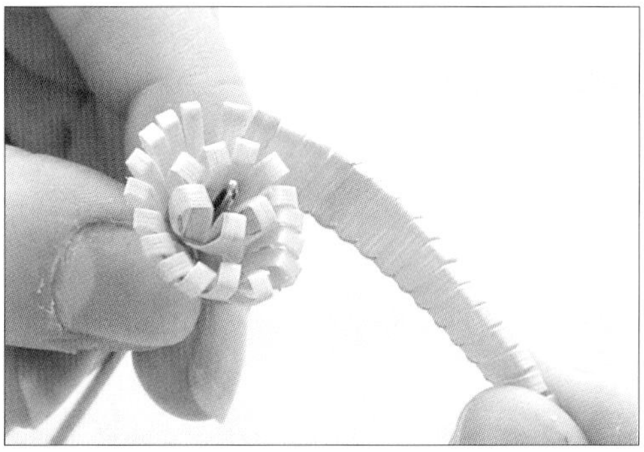

Making several rosettes

Traditionally the workers made long lengths of joined windings which they called worms (schlengge). They cut them off and finished them as and when required.

1. Follow the instructions to Finishing step 1, but this time wind the two wires to a length of 5cm (2"). Do not cut.

2. Slide the first length down the form. Make a second length, following the instructions from Starting step 5.

Passementerie

Hop (Hopfen)

The splints must be very fine, less than 1mm wide. They are prepared in a way that keeps them together so that they can be worked as one. Before you begin take note of the following points. Avoid pulling the wire too tightly around each group (it might cut through the splints). Use long splints so that you do not have to join (joining will spoil the appearance of the finished motif).

You will need:

>   Prepared splints 46cm (18")
>   Form, 12mm (0.5") wide and 1mm thick
>   Darning needle
>   Wire cutters

Starting

1. Choose a splitter that has sufficient fins to cut the whole straw into splints less than 1mm wide.
2. Split the straw to 12mm (0.5") from the end. Withdraw the splitter leaving the end of the straw whole.
3. Split open the whole straw section and then flatten it. See photograph shown below.

4. Carefully soften the splints.
5. Start by using the rosette method. Fasten the un-split end between the wires, keep the shiny upwards. *(Fig. 45)*

Fig. 45

Working

1. Use the rosette method to make a 6cm (2.5") length.

Finishing

1. Fasten the end of the splint in the wires, twist the wires together and then cut them leaving a 5cm (2") length.
2. Hold the twisted wires at the pointed end of the needle with the ends hanging downwards.
3. Wind the work around the needle and wires, in a spiral movement. The fold of the splints should just cover the wired edge. *(Fig. 46)*

Fig. 46

4. Fasten the ends by twisting together the two sets of wires. Trim the splint ends.

Split slowly and carefully, then open the end with a sharp knife.

Winding

Little Star (Sternli)

Although this motif is called a star, its shape is more like a flower. It is worked on a tool with pins set rather like a daisy winder and the technique is very similar. This motif can be made with split straw or with straw thread (Schnürli). For clarity the first diagram is marked as a clock face.

You will need:

> 1 splint 2mm wide, 31cm (12")
> Sternli tool
> Needle, optional

Starting

1. Lay the splint, shiny side uppermost, across the circle leaving an end of 5cm (2") protruding to the right of pin 6. As you work keep the shiny side up.

Working

1. Wind the working end around pin 12 from left to right. (*Fig. 47*)
2. Bring it down and around pin 6 from right to left. (*Fig. 48*)
3. Pass it around pin 2 from left to right. (*Fig. 49*)
4. Wind around pin 8. (*Fig. 50*)
5. Take it across to and around pin 4. (*Fig. 51*)
6. Finally wind around pin 10, from left to right. Lay working end between pins 4 and 6. (*Fig. 52*)

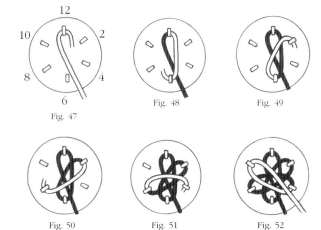

Fig. 47

Fig. 48

Fig. 49

Fig. 50

Fig. 51

Fig. 52

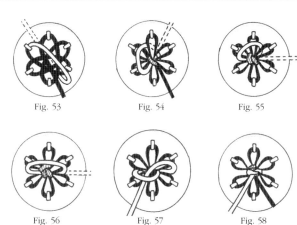

Fig. 53

Fig. 54

Fig. 55

Fig. 56

Fig. 57

Fig. 58

Finishing

1. Take the working end and pass it under all the work from between pins 4 and 6 to emerge between pins 10 and 12. Gently tighten. (*Fig. 53*)
2. Pass the end between pins 6 and 8 and under all the work to emerge from between pins 12 and 2. Tighten. (*Fig. 54*)
3. Pass the end between pins 8 and 10 to emerge between pins 2 and 4. Tighten. (*Fig. 55*)
4. Take the end across between pins 8 and 10 and then pass it under the work to emerge between 2 and 4. Leave a small loop. (*Fig. 56*)
5. Thread the end through the loop. (*Fig. 57*)
6. Tighten the first loop, and then tighten the second loop. (*Fig. 58*)
7. Carefully lift the motif off the pins.

Beads (Knöpfli or Kugeli)

Traditionally the machine produced bead or form was made from lime (linden), poplar or maple wood, and then hand wrapped with either a straw splint, Schnürli or very narrow Ring plait. Each shape, round, flat, hemi-spherical or teardrop had its own name; olive (Oliven), globes (Kugeli), little split straw bags (Halmentäschli) and peardrop or acorn (Strohbirli or Eicheli). When strung together as a fringe they were known as snowdrops (Grelot or locally as Gragöl). The beads are easy to make but do require patience and nimble fingers.

Basic Bead

Workers made them in a variety sizes from 2mm up to 20mm diameter. The splint width must be varied according to the size of form, but do not use one less than 1mm wide. A big form may need a splint 3mm wide, or wider. First practice the technique by covering a large, flat form with a wide splint. Once familiar, reduce the size of both the form and splint. As you wrap do not stop and look; make any adjustments once the form is covered and fastened.

You will need:

> Form, bead or washer, 12mm (0.5") diameter
> Straw splint, 3mm wide, 30cm (12")
> Darning needle, optional

Starting

1. Hold the splint with the pith side against the form.
2. Insert one end of the splint into the hole. *(Fig. 59)*
3. If there is no hole then hold the end against the form.

Fig. 59

Working

1. Wrap the splint once around the form, making sure that it is tight. *(Fig. 60)*
2. Make another wrap, this time taking the splint to one side of the previous wrapping. The edges must overlap.
3. Repeat the wrapping until the form is covered. *(Fig. 61)*

Fig. 60

Fig. 61

Finishing

1. Loosen the last wrap and thread the splint end under it, or use a needle and thread the needle point under the last two or three wraps. *(Fig. 62)*
2. Thread the splint end back under the loop and tighten. *(Fig. 63)*
3. Do not twist the splint on itself, a twisted splint will break when pulled.

Fig. 62

Fig. 63

Beaded hat ornament.

Beads (Knöpfli or Kugeli)

Peardrop (Strohbirli)

To make this shape you must use a form with a hole in the centre. I suggest that you practice the basic bead before moving on to this motif.

You will need:

Bead, 6mm (0.25") diameter
Piece of straw, thickness matching that of the hole in the form
Splint, 2mm wide, 40cm (16")
Darning needle

Starting

1. Put the stem into the form. Cut the stem to 12–15mm (0.5") long. The length must be proportionate to the size of form. *(Fig. 64)*

2. Hold the pith side of the splint under the form and poke the end into the straw. *(Fig. 65)*

Fig. 64

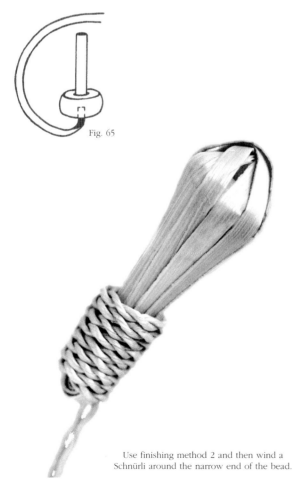

Fig. 65

Working

1. Follow the working sequence for the Basic Bead, but this time wrap the splint around the form and over the top of the stem. *(Fig. 66)*

Fig. 66

Finishing ~ method 1

1. Use the Finishing method for the Basic Bead.

Finishing ~ method 2

1. Carefully thread the end of the splint through a needle eye and pass it through the central straw stem, from the wide bottom end to top. Make sure the needle and end pass through all the layers of top windings. *(Fig. 67)*

Fig. 67

Finishing ~ method 3

1. Thread the splint through the central stem from narrow end to the wide end. *(Fig. 68)*

Fig. 68

Use finishing method 2 and then wind a Schnürli around the narrow end of the bead.

Figure of Eight with two working ends

This section introduces the technique of sequence winding around needles, known by the Swiss workers as Fork Work (Gabelarbeiten). The winding sequence can take a little time to learn, so be prepared to practice. To make the instructions easier to follow the needles have been numbered from left to right, 1, 2, 3.

Shovel (Schüfeli)

The original motifs were made by winding very narrow splints around short thin needles that were placed 3mm apart. I suggest that you begin by using wider splints, thicker needles and a wider spacing. To ensure that the finished motif has its traditional shiny appearance each splint must be twisted as you work, so follow the diagrams.

You will need:

> 2 splints 2mm wide 46cm (18")
> 3 needles set 5mm (0.25") apart into a holder
> Insert the centre needle (2) into the holder with eye downwards

Starting

1. Put the two narrowest ends of both splints between needles 1 and 2, pith sides against the holder. The short ends, approximately 12mm (0.5"), must be at the front, and the long ends at the back. *(Fig. 69)*

2. Hold the short ends in place.

3. Work the left-hand splint, shaded in the diagrams, around needles 1 and 2. Wind it around the outside of needle 1 so that it is at the front. Pass it to the back between needles 1 and 2. Wind it to the front around needle 2. Pull the end across the front to lay to the left of needle 1 and hold in place. Note how the splint twists as the splint is wound. *(Fig. 70)*

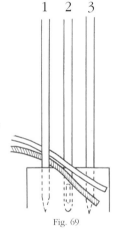

Fig. 69

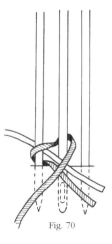

Fig. 70

4. Work the second splint. Bring it to the front, between needles 1 and 2. Take it across the front of needle 2, and then behind needle 3. Wind it around the outside of needle 3, and then take it to the back, between needles 3 and 2. Wind it around needle 2 to the front. Pull the end to the right of needle 3 and hold in place. Note how the splint twists. *(Fig. 71)*

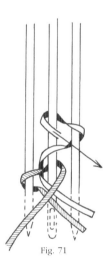

Fig. 71

Working

1. Pass the left-hand splint between needles 1 and 2 to the back. Wind it around needle 1 to the front. Pass it between needles 1 and 2 to the back. Wind it around needle 2; pull the end to the front to lay in front of needle 1.

2. Work the second splint. Pass it between needles 2 and 3 to the back. Wind it around needle 3 to the front. Pass it between needles 3 and 2, then around needle 2 to the front. Pull it to the right of needle 3 and hold in place.

Figure of Eight with two working ends

3. Repeat Working steps 1 and 2 until there are 14 moves on each side. Finish on working step 1. To make the finishing moves there must be 5cm (2") of each splint left unused.

Finishing

1. The splints must be damp. Thread the top, left-hand splint into needle 1 and the lower, right-hand splint into needle 3. *(Fig. 72)*

2. Carefully remove all the needles from the holder. Pull needles 1 and 3 downward through the windings so that the splints pass through them. Pull gently to tighten the splints against the last stitches. Remove needles 1 and 3.

3. Push needle 2 upwards, and thread the two splint ends, which were just pulled through the windings, through the needle eye. *(Fig. 73)*

4. Gently pull needle 2 through the central windings, unthread and remove the needle. *(Fig. 74)*

5. Pull the long splint ends and the top stitches will curve toward the centre. Trim the short ends. Gently ease the loops to create a curved top and make any adjustments while the motif is still damp.

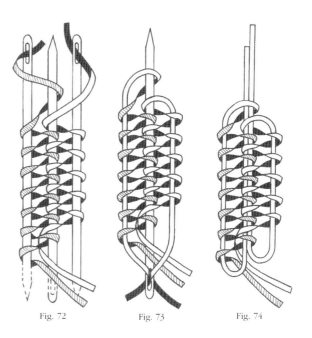

Fig. 72   Fig. 73   Fig. 74

> **Handy hint**
> *Only thread about 6mm (0.25") of the splint through the eyes of the needles. This prevents the ends becoming entangled in the stitches.*

Twist the splint to keep the shiny side facing outwards.

Figure of Eight with two working ends

Small Half Moon (Halbmöndli)

This motif looks very pretty when made with very narrow splints and a lot of windings but to achieve this you need to use very long splints. Alternatively join two shorter splints with a Weaver's Knot, page 73. The splints must be wound with the shiny side outwards.

You will need:

2 lengths of splint 2mm wide, 46cm (18")
3 needles spaced 5mm (0.25") apart in a holder
The left and centre needles (1 and 2) must be fixed with the eyes upwards, and the right-hand needle (3) with the eye downwards

Starting

1. Place one splint, with the pith side against the holder, between needles 1 and 2. Keep the short end at the front. Wind the long end around the outside of needle 1, then pass it to the back between needles 1 and 2. Wind it around the outside of needle 2 and pull it across the front of the holder to lay to the left of needle 1. (*Fig. 75*)

2. Add the second splint, sliding it under the previous windings. Keep the short end at the front. Pass the long end diagonally across the front of needle 2, and then pass it between needles 2 and 3 to the back. Wind it around the outside of needle 3, and then pass it between needles 3 and 2 to the back.

Small Half Moon motifs decorated with straw beads.

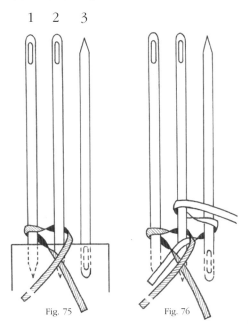

Fig. 75   Fig. 76

Wind the end around the outside of needle 2, and then pull it across the front of the holder to lay to the right of needle 3. (*Fig. 76*)

Working

1. Follow the working instructions for the Shovel motif, making about 17 windings, counted on needle 1. The number of stitches will depend upon the length of splints, there must be 2cm (1") of unused splint for finishing.

Figure of Eight with two working ends

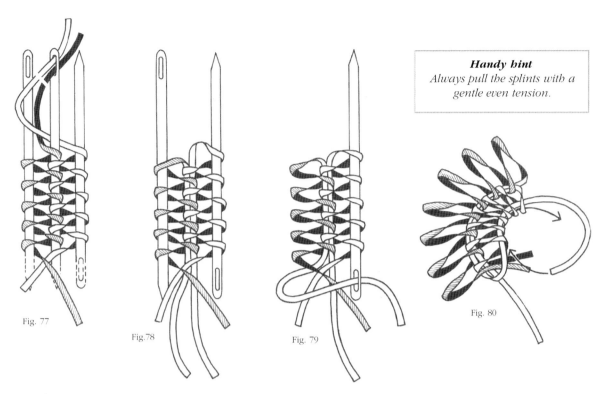

> **Handy hint**
> *Always pull the splints with a gentle even tension.*

Fig. 77

Fig.78

Fig. 79

Fig. 80

Finishing

1. Thread both ends through needle 2. *(Fig. 77)*

2. Carefully remove all the needles from the holder.

3. Pull needle 2 downwards through the stitches so that both splints are threaded through the windings. *(Fig. 78)*

4. Unthread the needle and remove needle 1.

5. Thread the long end of the right-hand splint through the eye of needle 3. Both short starting ends of the splints must lay between the long ends of splints. *(Fig. 79)*

6. Pull the needle through the stitches then unthread.

7. Carefully thread a needle through the right-hand row of stitches (the row that the needle and splint have just been pulled through). Thread the splint end in the eye and pull through. Unthread the needle. *(Fig. 80)*

8. Ease the motif into a semi-circle by pulling gently on each end in turn. Arrange the 'petals'.

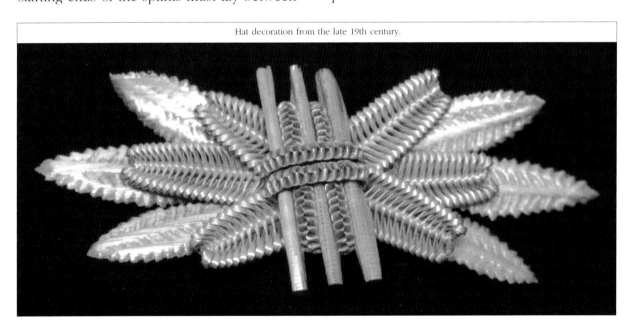

Hat decoration from the late 19th century.

STRAW THREAD

Preparation

Straw threads are narrow splints twisted together into a fine two-ply thread usually between 35 and 40cm (14" to 16") long. To prevent confusion in the instructions they are always referred to by their Swiss name Schnürli (little strings).

Some motifs have strange and intriguing names, which although known to their makers would not have been known by those who proudly wore them on their hats. Archival evidence in the Freiämter Stroh Museum shows that the dealers in Wohlen changed some names for sales purposes; the Rat Dropping became Worm, and the Bedbug became a Little Thread Leaf.

Selecting straw

Wheat is suitable but rye straw splints make the strongest Schnürli.

Selecting splints

Use thoroughly softened, damp splints that are free of cracks and blemishes. The width of the splints will determine the thickness of the finished Schnürli. The length of the splints will determine the length of the Schnürli.

Dampening

Unless stated otherwise, the Schnürli must be worked whilst damp. Dip them into warm water, no hotter than hand-hot, until they are dampened, no longer than a minute. Do not leave Schnürli standing in water; they will lose their colour, weaken and may unwind. You may have to re-dampen as you work, use a spray to mist the working section.

Before you begin

Unless otherwise stated, needles have been placed approximately 5mm (0.25") apart and the suggested working length of Schnürli in each set of instructions has been based on this arrangement.

The diagrams do not necessarily show all completed moves and when you see a break in the diagram it indicates that not all the length is shown.

Imperial measurements are usually approximate.

You may need to adjust the spacing between needles and the number of stitches when using other textile threads.

Making Schnürli

Basic Schnürli

You will need a spinning machine (Schnürlirädli) since although these threads can be made by hand the machine is much faster.

You will need:

> 2 damp prepared splints 1–2mm wide, at least 40cm (16")

Starting

1. Attach the wider end of each single splint to the hook of each spindle. *(Fig. 81)*

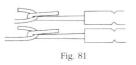

Fig. 81

Working

1. Gently grip the splints using your thumb and first finger to keep them separate. Turn the wheel at a constant speed whilst slowly drawing your hand away from the hooks. The flat splints will turn on themselves. Do not over spin; the twists should be loose and even. *(Fig. 82)*

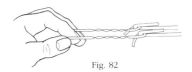

Fig. 82

2. Without letting go of the splints (they will undo!) hook both into the single hook on the left-hand part of the machine. *(Fig. 83)*

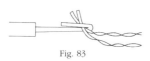

Fig. 83

3. The splints may start to twist together. Gently separate them back to the hook and insert the first finger of your left hand between them. *(Fig. 84)*

Fig. 84

4. Start turning the wheel in the same direction as before and slowly move your finger towards the right until the whole length is twisted. Remove your finger. *(Fig. 85)*

Fig. 85

Finishing

1. Hook both splints on to one of the hooks on the right-hand end of the machine. Gently hold the twisted thread between the thumb and first finger of your left hand. Tighten the ply by turning the wheel in the opposite direction and whilst gently pressing the Schnürli move your thumb and finger slowly toward the left. *(Fig. 86)*

2. Remove the Schnürli from the hooks.

Fig. 86

Variation

Use dyed splints to make coloured Schnürli. Mix dyed and natural splints to make multi-coloured Schnürli.

Add a fine metallic thread or coloured thread to either one or both splints during Working step 1.

Add a decorative thread during Working step 3, allowing it to twist into the ply as you spin.

Making Schnürli

COMMON PROBLEMS

If the ply is uneven:

The speed at which you move your finger in Working step 4 controls the tightening of the thread.

If the Schnürli keep breaking:

The splint may be damaged.
Adjust the speed at which you turn the wheel.
Straw will snap if over-wound.

If the two splints will not ply together:

Check the weight, it must be adjusted according to the type of straw and width of splint being spun.
The weight must be free to spin during working, use nylon line.

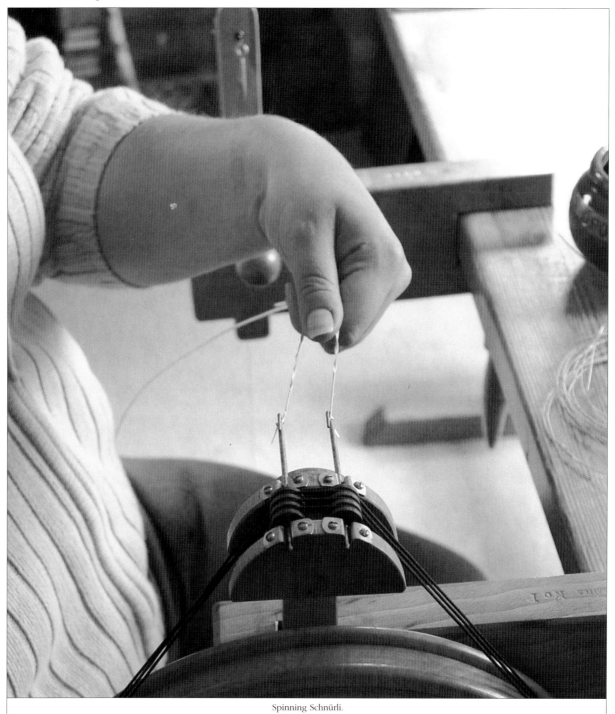

Spinning Schnürli.

Making Schnürli

MAKING HORSEHAIR SCHNÜRLI

These are made by spinning together either 4 or 6 hairs at least 40cm (16") long, matched for thickness and divided into two equal groups. Follow instructions for making straw Schnürli, remembering to first dampen the hairs. Since horsehair Schnürli have a tendency to unwind, clip or make a simple knot at each end.

Straw and Horsehair Schnürli on a horsehair and silk Bordüre.

MAKING SCHNÜRLI BY HAND

Tape or clamp two prepared splints to a firm surface. Twist the right-hand splint twice in a clockwise direction. Move it over the top of the left-hand splint and hold in the left-hand.

Put the original left-hand splint in your right-hand. Twist the new right-hand splint twice and move it over the top of the left-hand splint to your left hand; put the splint in your right hand into your left hand. Put the left-hand splint in your right hand. Continue the movements until you reach the end of the splints. Secure the ends until dry.

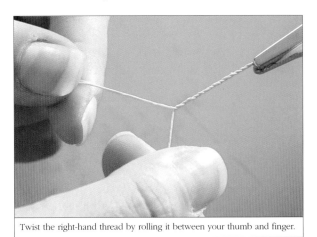

Twist the right-hand thread by rolling it between your thumb and finger.

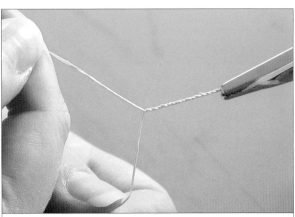

Hold the splints taut as you take the right-hand splint over to the left.

Winding

By winding around forms of various sizes it is possible to vary the size. If you make more windings or use a large diameter form you will have to increase the recommended length of Schnürli. The winding must be rhythmic and at a constant tension; as you wind take care not to unwind the ply of the Schnürli.

 urls

Balance the proportions of the motif by adjusting the number of windings according to the thickness of the form.

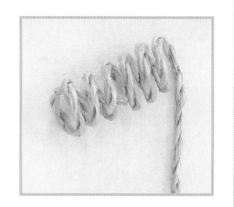

You will need:

> Schnürli 15cm (6")
> Form such as cable or wicking needle
> Plastic bag tie

Starting

1. Hold 15mm (0.7") of one end alongside the form. *(Fig. 87)*

Working

1. Start winding the long end around the form and over the end working back towards the short end. *(Fig. 88)*

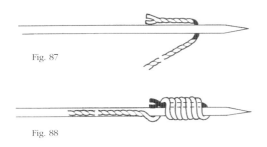

Fig. 87

Fig. 88

2. Make about 8 windings.
3. Secure the ends and leave until dry.

Finishing

1. Gently slide off the form. Trim the short end. The long end is the stem. Once dry it will hold its shape

Variation

Make tapered curls by winding around the point of a skewer or cable needle. *(Fig. 89)*

Fig. 89

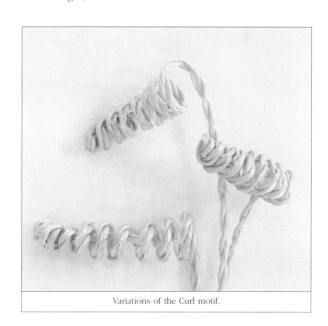

Variations of the Curl motif.

Winding

Rat Dropping or Worm (Rattenchegel or Würm)

Traditionally the Schnürli is wound directly around a straw or around a matchstick with a thin large-eye needle placed alongside. The ends of this motif are rounded.

You will need:

> Schnürli, damp 25cm (10")
> Straw stem 5cm (2")
> Darning or crewel needle

Starting

1. Put the needle inside the straw stem.
2. Lay 2.5cm (1") of the Schnürli along the stem The end is by the eye of the needle. *(Fig. 90)*

Working

1. Wind about 16 times around the straw stem and over the end of the Schnürli, working back toward the needle eye. Remember to leave a short end of Schnürli uncovered. *(Fig. 91)*
2. Thread the long end of the Schnürli through the needle. *(Fig. 92)*

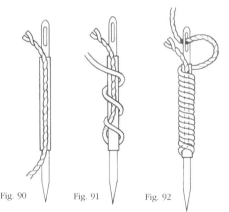

Fig. 90　　Fig. 91　　Fig. 92

Finishing

1. Pull the needle through the stem. *(Fig. 93)*
2. The Schnürli will cut through the stem. Unthread the needle.
3. Gently pull on both Schnürli ends so that the ends of the windings become rounded.
4. Pull the Schnürli ends to one side and trim each end of the stem to within 2mm of the winding. Pull the Schnürli back into the centre of the stem.
5. To correct the shape, roll the motif between your fingers.
6. Trim one end of the Schnürli, the other end is the stem.

Fig. 93

> **Handy hint**
> *Only work with the twisted part of the Schnürli, the untwisted ends are weak.*

Mouse Dropping (Mausechegel)

This motif is much smaller than the Rat Dropping and is made by winding a 10cm (4") length of Schnürli 5 or 6 times directly around the needle. Vary the size by using a thicker Schnürli and increasing the number of windings.

Winding

Small Pan Ball (Pfannerugeli)

This motif is sometimes called Frying Pan. Take care with the winding since neatness is very important.

You will need:

Schnürli, damp 23cm (10")
Darning or wicking needle
Thread, optional

Starting

1. Thread 5cm (2") of Schnürli through the eye of the needle.

Working

1. Wind the Schnürli around the needle until 5cm (2") of the Schnürli remains, approximately 20 windings.

Finishing

1. Adjust the threaded end of Schnürli so only 15mm (0.6") is threaded through the eye.
2. Put the other end through the loop.
(Fig. 94)

3. Pull the needle through until the loop disappears into the windings. *(Fig. 95)*

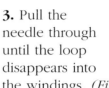
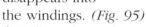
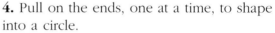

Fig. 94

4. Pull on the ends, one at a time, to shape into a circle.
5. You may secure by tying together the ends of the Schnürli or tie with fine straw coloured thread.

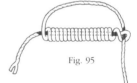

Fig. 95

This bonnet trimming incorporates Small Pan Ball motifs, Schnürli Beads, Straw beads and Bögli.

Winding

Air Ball (Luftrugeli)

As the name indicates this motif is a puffy rounded motif, made by winding the Schnürli around two needles. The size can be adjusted by using thicker needles.

You will need:

> Schnürli 30cm (12") long
> 2 wicking needles

Starting

1. Hold two needles so that they are side by side and touching. The eyes are at the top.
2. Thread 3cm (1.5") of the Schnürli through the left-hand eye. *(Fig. 96)*

Working

1. Wind the Schnürli around both needles leaving a 3cm (1.5") length for finishing.
2. Pull the threaded end back through the needle eye so that only 10mm (0.5") remains threaded. *(Fig. 97)*

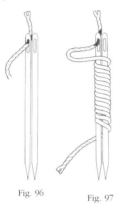

Fig. 96

Fig. 97

Handy hint

Make the motif more circular by threading the end (Finishing step 4) through the centre of the windings so that it emerges further around the circle.

Air Ball variations.

Finishing

1. Pull the threaded needle through the centre of the windings then unthread the needle. *(Fig. 98)*
2. Thread the same end through the eye of the second needle. It must pass behind the unthreaded end. *(Fig. 99)*
3. Pull the needle through the windings and then unthread.
4. Pull the end that comes through the centre of the windings to form a circle. *(Fig. 100)*
5. Trim this end so that it is hidden in the windings. The second end forms a stem.

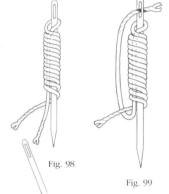

Fig. 98

Fig. 99

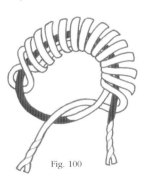

Fig. 100

Variation

This motif can also be made with splints or with Schnürli that have been unwound. By winding around an extra needle every few windings it is possible to make a looped Air Ball.

Winding

Schnürli Bead (Drähtli Knöpfli)

For this motif two Schnürli are wound side by side. A smaller form would require only one Schnürli whilst a larger one would require three.

You will need:

1 form 10mm diameter (compressed cotton, wood or plastic beads with a hole large enough for the needle to pass through)
2 Schnürli 40cm (16")
1 cotton thread 18cm (7")
Darning or crewel needle

Starting

1. Fold the cotton thread in half and thread through the form. *(Fig. 101)*

2. Bring the ends to the top and thread them back through the hole. Adjust so that they are on opposite sides. *(Fig. 102)*

3. Thread the Schnürli through the cotton loop. *(Fig. 103)*

4. Pull the ends of cotton to tighten the loop and pull the Schnürli ends into the hole. Grip the form by holding the cotton ends. Keep the threads at opposite sides of the form.

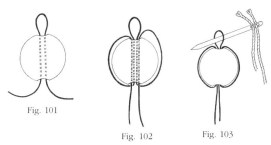

Fig. 101

Fig. 102   Fig. 103

Working

1. Simultaneously wind the two Schnürli around the form taking them under each cotton thread. *(Fig. 104)*

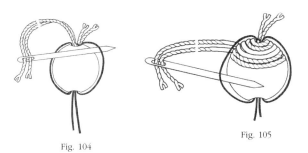

Fig. 104

Fig. 105

A decoration combining Schnürli beads and Oberwil Rosettes.

2. The Schnürli must lie neatly side by side. Keep them in place by pulling gently on the ends of the cotton thread. *(Fig. 105)*

3. Keep winding until the form is covered.

Finishing

1. Knot the cotton around the ends of Schnürli then thread the ends of Schnürli through the centre of the form. *(Fig. 106)*

2. Trim the ends of cotton and the short ends of Schnürli. Leave the longer ends as a stem.

Fig. 106

Interlocking Loops

This section is the first step towards more complex motifs. The Schnürli is twisted and threaded into interlocking loops. Both techniques in this section can be used to make a length of decorative edging in which case it will be necessary to join lengths of Schnürli together by using a Weaver's knot, see opposite page.

Carpet Beater (Teppichklopfer)

Start by making this motif with one Schnürli then once you feel confident work two simultaneously, and then work three side by side.

You will need:
>   Schnürli 30cm (12")
>   Thread

Starting

1. Hold one end of the Schnürli in the left hand.

Working

1. Twist the other end so that it forms a loop with the long end crossing over about 5cm (2") from the left-hand end of the Schnürli. *(Fig. 107)*

2. Make a second loop by passing the end through the first loop from front to back. Bring it to the front passing it over the bottom of the second loop. *(Fig. 108)*

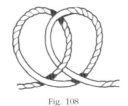

Fig. 107   Fig. 108

3. Adjust the loop so that it matches the size of the first.

4. Continue making loops until a total of either 5 or 7 have been made. *(Fig. 109)*

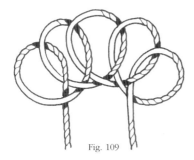

Fig. 109

Finishing

1. Bring together the two ends and tie with thread to secure. *(Fig. 110)*

2. The shape of the motif can be varied according to where the tie is made.

Fig. 110

Variation

Increase the loop size making the centre one the largest and then reduce the size to match the first.

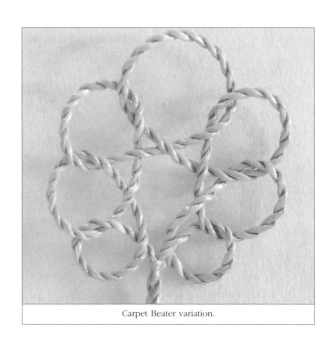

Carpet Beater variation.

Interlocking Loops

Carpet Beater Leaf (Teppichklopfer Blatt)

This time the loops are worked as opposites. By adjusting the size of loop you will affect the final shape.

You will need:
>   Schnürli 35cm (14")
>   Thread

Starting

1. Take the Schnürli and fold in half crossing the left-hand end over the right-hand end. *(Fig. 107)*

Working

1. Take the right-hand length and make a second loop by passing the end through the first loop from front to back. Bring it back toward you over the bottom of the loop. *(Fig. 108)*

2. Take the left-hand length and make a third loop by passing the end through the first loop from back to front and then out under the bottom of the loop. *(Fig. 111)*

3. Adjust the size of the loops.

4. Cross the two long ends with the left-hand Schnürli passing over the right. *(Fig. 112)*

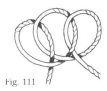
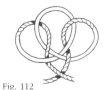

Fig. 111   Fig. 112

5. Continue making loops first right, then left, then cross the ends until the leaf is sufficiently long.

Finishing

1. Cross the ends of the Schnürli and tie with thread.

Variation

Adjust the size by tightening or loosening the threads where they cross over, Working step 5.

WEAVER'S KNOT (SHEET BEND)

As you begin to make larger motifs you will need to join Schnürli using a flat secure knot.

a   b

c   d

Carpet Beater variations including decorative edgings.

Half Hitch

The half hitch is one of the simplest knots and by introducing simple variations to the sequence it can be used to create a large range of motifs.

Centime or Penny (Räppli)

As the name suggests this is a small motif. Working from one end of the Schnürli it is made by working a row of half hitches.

You will need:

Schnürli 30cm (12")
Darning or wicking needle

Starting

1. Hold the needle eye downwards.
2. Hold about 5cm (2") of the Schnürli alongside the needle, this is needed to finish the motif.

Working

1. Make a loop with the long end crossing over the front of the loop.
2. Put the loop behind the needle and then drop it over. (*Fig. 113*)
3. Take the long end and make a second half hitch exactly the same as the first. (*Fig. 114*)
4. Slide the half hitch down to meet the first and gently tighten by pulling the long end at a right angle to the needle.
5. Leave 5cm (2") of unworked Schnürli for finishing.

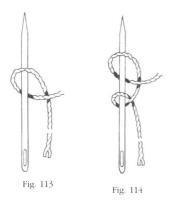

Fig. 113   Fig. 114

Finishing

1. Slide all the half hitches down the needle. Thread the short end of Schnürli through the eye of the needle leaving a loop. Take the other end behind the needle point then thread through the loop from front to back. (*Fig. 115*)
2. Pull the needle through the work, leaving a small loop at the end. (*Fig. 116*)

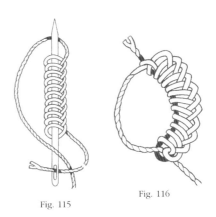

Fig. 115   Fig. 116

3. Lightly hold the stitches to prevent them turning inward. With an even tension pull on the loop and shape the stitches into a circle. Pull on the end that passes through the stitches. Flatten the motif with your fingers.
4. Once you are happy with the shape, pull on both ends to lock the last stitch.

> ***Handy hint***
> *Do not push the end of the Schnürli*
> *too far through the eye of the needle.*
> *A long end can get caught in the stitches.*

Half Hitch

TWO-NEEDLE CENTIME

This larger version of the Centime is made around two needles. It requires a longer length of Schnürli since you will make about 15 stitches. The needles can be hand-held so that they touch, or put into a needle holder with a space of about 3mm between them. Turn the needles so that the eye of the right-hand needle is at the top and the eye of the left-hand needle is at the bottom. *(Fig. 117)*

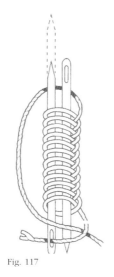

Fig. 117

Two-needle Centime.

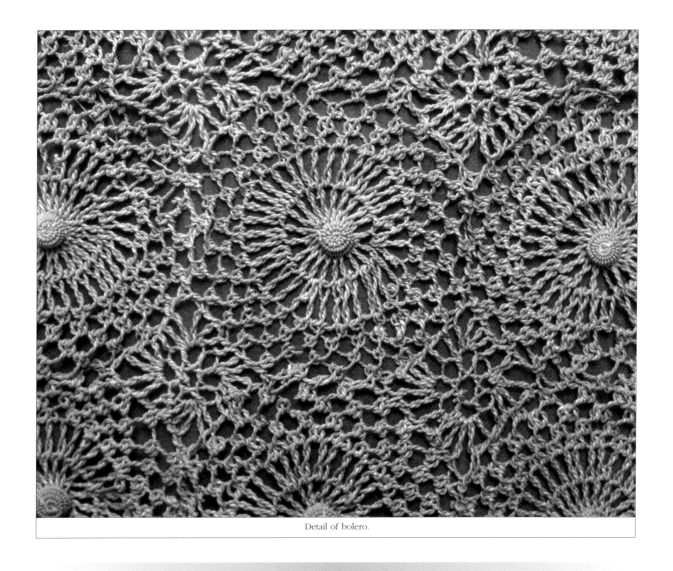

Detail of bolero.

Half Hitch

Bedbug or Small Thread Leaf (Wäntele or Schnürliblättli)

This time start working in the middle of the Schnürli and make half hitches with both ends. Do take care and follow the diagrams otherwise the motif will twist.

You will need:
>   Schnürli 35cm (14")
>   Crewel, darning or wicking needle

Starting

1. Hold the needle eye uppermost.
2. Put the mid-point of the Schnürli horizontally in front of the needle. Hold in place.

Working

1. Use the right-hand end to make a half hitch. *(Fig. 118)*
2. Tighten by pulling the end to the right.
3. Make a half hitch with the end on the left-hand side. This half hitch mirrors the first. *(Fig. 119)*

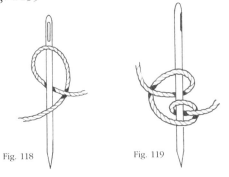

Fig. 118   Fig. 119

4. Slide the stitch down the needle and tighten by pulling to the left.
5. Leave 4cm (1.75") of unworked Schnürli for finishing.

Finishing

1. Thread both ends through the eye of the needle. *(Fig. 120)*
2. Pull the needles downwards through the stitches.
3. Whilst still damp adjust the shape.

Fig. 120

Variation

Shape the leaf by increasing the width of half hitches in the centre section.

TWO-NEEDLE BEDBUG

This is a bigger version so you may need to use a longer length of Schnürli. For ease of working the needles can be put into a holder. The only variation is in the final threading. *(Fig. 121)*

Fig. 121

Two-needle Bedbug.

> ***Handy hint***
> *Do not pull the half hitches too tight, it will be difficult to pull them off the needle.*

Half Hitch

Looped Leaf (Blatt)

The left-hand needle acts as a spacer and by adjusting the gap between the two you can increase or decrease the size of loop.

You will need:

Schnürli 63cm (25")
2 darning or wicking needles
Needle holder

Starting

1. Fix the needles, points downwards, into the holder 6mm (0.25") apart.
2. Measure 25cm (10") from one end of the Schnürli and hold in front of the right-hand needle with the longer end pointing to the left.

Working

1. Start working with the shorter right-hand end and make a half hitch on the right-hand needle.
2. Use the left-hand end to make a half hitch around both needles. (*Fig. 122*)
3. Leave 5cm (2") of unworked Schnürli for finishing.

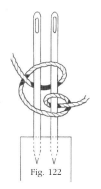

Fig. 122

Finishing

1. Thread both ends through the right-hand needle. (*Fig. 123*)
2. Remove the needles from the holder. Pull them downwards through the loops.
3. Shape whilst still damp.

Fig. 123

> **Handy hint**
> *If two Schnürli have been knotted together keep the knot against the right-hand needle.*

FLOWER

Follow the instructions for the Looped Leaf. Put the extra needle through the final loop, with the eye pointing to the right (*Fig. 124*). Pull both original needles downwards through the stitches until the loop grips the remaining needle. Unthread the original needles. Thread the Schnürli ends through the eye of the needle and pull through the loops (*Fig. 125*). Unthread the needle. Pull on the ends to tighten the loops so that they almost disappear into the body of the motif. Pull into a circle using your fingers to flatten the motif at the same time.

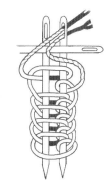

Fig. 124

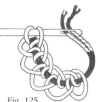

Fig. 125

Flower.

Half Hitch

Needle Rose (Nadelrösli)

So far the half hitches have been worked in the same direction, but the for the next three motifs you must make them as a pair.

You will need:
> Schnürli 35cm (14")
> 2 wicking needles

Starting

1. Hold one needle with the eye pointing downwards.
2. Hold the Schnürli 5cm (2") from the left-hand end.

Working

1. Use the long end to make a half hitch with the end passing <u>over</u> the right-hand side. Put the loop behind the needle and drop it over the point. Pull it down the needle and gently tighten by pulling the end to the right. (*Fig. 126*)

Fig. 126

2. Make a second half hitch with the end passing <u>under</u> the right-hand side. Place in front of the needle and drop it down. Pull the end sideways and tighten. (*Fig. 127*)
3. Leave 4cm (1.5") of unworked Schnürli for finishing.

Fig. 127

Finishing

1. Slide the work down the needle and thread the short end of the Schnürli through the eye of the needle.
2. Put the second needle through the loop with the eye pointing to the left. (*Fig. 128*)
3. Pull the threaded needle through the motif. Unthread.

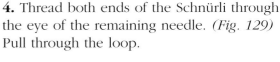

4. Thread both ends of the Schnürli through the eye of the remaining needle. (*Fig. 129*) Pull through the loop.

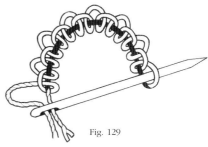

Fig. 129

5. Keep the loops between the linked half hitches to the outside and shape by pulling on the ends.

Variation

Make a larger motif by using two or three needles held side by side.

CATERPILLAR (RÄUPLI)

Follow the instructions up to Working step 3. Follow Finishing step 1 and then pull the threaded needle through the stitches, gently tightening the last stitch.

Fig. 128

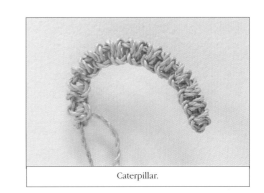

Caterpillar.

Half Hitch

Springtime by Brigitte Koch-Berger, Bremgarten, Switzerland.

Half Hitch

Five-petal Rose

Although this motif is simple to make it requires concentration; the sequence is more complex. Do persevere and be patient during the final threading, it's worth it as the motif is very pretty.

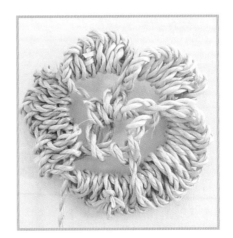

You will need:

Schnürli, damp 120cm (47")
2 wicking needles
Needle holder
1 or 2 crewel or darning needles
Kebab stick or knitting needle
Pin board, optional

Starting

1. Put the eye of the left-hand needle and the point of the right-hand needle in the holder so that they almost touch.
2. Fold the Schnürli 10cm (4") from the right-hand end. Place the fold behind the left-hand needle with the long end to the left. Hold the short end against the holder. *(Fig. 132)*

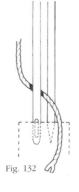

Fig. 132

Working

1. Make two half hitches around the left-hand needle then put the long end behind the right-hand needle. *(Fig. 133)*
2. Make a half hitch around the right-hand needle. It is worked in the opposite direction to the first two. *(Fig. 134)*

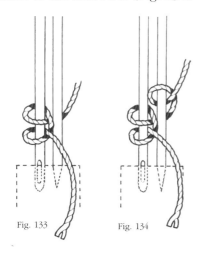

Fig. 133   Fig. 134

3. Repeat Working step 2 until there are a total of twelve half hitches on the right-hand needle.
4. Pass the Schnürli between the two needles to lay behind the left-hand needle. *(Fig. 135)*
5. Repeat Working steps 1 to 4 until there are 5 sets of left-hand half hitches and 5 sets of twelve right-hand half hitches. Finish the working sequence on the last stitch of the group of twelve.
6. There must be 5cm (2") of unworked Schnürli for finishing.

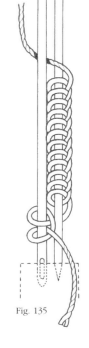

Fig. 135

Finishing

1. Carefully remove the needles from the holder.
2. Thread the left-hand thread (bottom) through the left-hand needle and the right-hand thread (top) through the right-hand needle.
3. Put a needle between the Schnürli and the left-hand needle. Pull the threaded needle through the stitches, then unthread. Tighten the loop against the extra needle.

Half Hitch

4. Thread the Schnürli into the extra needle and pull it through the loop. The flower centre will be finished later.

5. Put an extra needle between the Schnürli and the right-hand needle. Carefully and slowly pull the threaded needle through the work. Tighten the thread against the extra needle.

6. Thread the Schnürli into the eye of the extra needle and pull through.

7. Finish tightening the centre. Put a stick or knitting needle in the very centre to form a ring. Arrange the petals around.

8. Secure by tying the two ends of thread together. This pulls the final petal to the centre ring.

9. Pull or pin the petals to shape.

Five-petal Roses, Centimes, Rat Droppings and Bedbugs combined to make a fantastic trimming.

Figure of Eight with one working end

Make the motifs in this section by starting at one end of the Schnürli, working figure of eight movements around the needles and then joining the two ends.

Wagon Wheel (Wagerad)

This semicircular motif combines winding around one needle with a figure of eight stitch around both.

You will need:

Schnürli 45cm (18")
2 wicking or darning needles
Needle holder

Starting

1. Fix the eye ends of both needles into the holder with a gap of 6mm (0.25") between them.
2. Hold a 5cm (2") end against the needle holder.
3. Pass the long end to the back between the needles and then wind it anti-clockwise around the left-hand needle.

Working

1. Pass the long end between the needles to lay behind the right-hand needle.
2. Wind it around to the front of the right-hand needle then pass it between the needles to lay behind the left-hand needle. *(Fig. 136)*
3. Wind the Schnürli in an anti-clockwise direction four times around the left-hand needle.
4. Repeat until there are 6 figure of eight stitches and 6 sets of windings.

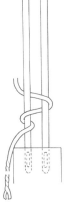

Fig. 136

Finishing

1. Remove the needles from the holder.
2. Slide the winding down the needles towards the eye. Thread the short end through the eye of the left-hand needle. *(Fig. 137)*
3. Gently pull the threaded needle through the left-hand windings. Leave the right-hand needle in place.
4. Thread both ends through the eye of the right-hand needle, making sure that one end is in front and one is behind the needle. *(Fig. 138)*
5. Pull the needle through the stitches.
6. Pull on each end in turn to create a semicircle.

Fig. 137

Fig. 138

Figure of Eight with one working end

Figure of Eight Rose (8-er Rösli)

Small is best with this motif so do use the recommended needle spacing. It can be made as a circular flower with either an open or closed centre or it can be pulled into a semicircle.

You will need:

> Schnürli 46cm (18")
> 3 wicking or darning needles
> Needle holder, optional

Starting

1. Thread a needle and pull through 5cm (2") of Schnürli.
2. Take a second needle and hold it above the threaded needle so that they are almost touching.

Working

1. Take the long Schnürli end between the two needles from front to back.
2. Wind it over the top needle to the front.
3. Pass the end between the two needles to the back.
4. Then wind around the bottom needle to the front. *(Fig. 139)*

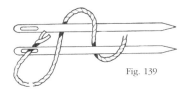

Fig. 139

5. Repeat Working steps 1 to 4 until there are sixteen stitches around the top needle.
6. Finish by winding the Schnürli around the lower needle. *(Fig. 140)*

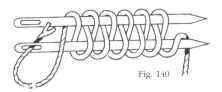

Fig. 140

Finishing

1. Adjust the threaded end of Schnürli so that only 6mm (0.25") is through the eye.
2. Thread the second end through the same needle.
3. Put the third needle through the loops. *(Fig. 141)*

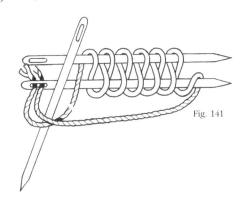

Fig. 141

4. Pull the threaded needle through the stitches, tighten the loops against the third needle then unthread the needle.
5. Remove the right-hand needle.
6. Re-thread the ends into the remaining needle.
7. Pull the needle through the loop and gently tighten by pulling the ends.

Figure of Eight with one working end

Panicle (Rispe)

The winding sequence is the same as the Figure of Eight Rose, but this time the configuration of the needles and final threading creates a compact leaf-like motif.

You will need:

>Schnürli 46cm (18")
>2 wicking or darning needles
>Needle holder, optional

Starting

1. The eye of the right-hand needle and point of the left-hand needle can be hand held or fixed into a holder. Space the needles about 6mm (0.25") apart.
2. Thread 5cm (2") of the end of Schnürli through the eye of the right-hand needle.

Working

1. Wind the Schnürli around the two needles in a figure of eight pattern. *(Fig. 142)*
2. Make eighteen complete moves.

Finishing

1. Thread the working end through the eye of the left-hand needle. *(Fig. 143)*
2. Pull the right-hand needle through the stitches.
3. Unthread the needle and re-thread the end through the left-hand needle. *(Fig. 144)*
4. Pull the needle through the stitches. *Fig. 145)*
5. Pull gently on both ends to curve the end.

This branch is made from shaped Bedbug motifs, but you could use Panicles.

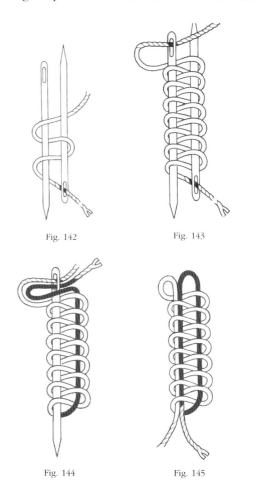

Fig. 142

Fig. 143

Fig. 144

Fig. 145

Figure of Eight with one working end

Flower

This motif is made in the same way as the Panicle, but is finished by threading the ends so that the stitches can be pulled into a flower shape.

You will need:
> Schnürli 92cm (36")
> 2 wicking or darning needles
> Needle holder, optional

Starting

1. Follow steps 1 and 2 of the Starting instructions for making a Panicle.

Working

1. Work at least twenty-two complete stitches.

Finishing

1. Follow the Panicle Finishing steps 1 to 3 and then use the following instructions.
2. Put a needle through the loops. *(Fig. 146)*
3. Pull both ends through the work. Unthread then rethread the ends into the eye of the remaining needle. *(Fig. 147)*
4. Pull the two ends through. Pull on the ends to tighten the loops and arrange into a flower.

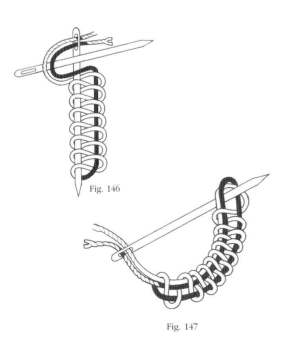

Fig. 146

Fig. 147

Variation

Put a cable knitting needle alongside the right-hand needle as you work the flower to create attractive puffy loops. You will need a longer length of Schnürli.

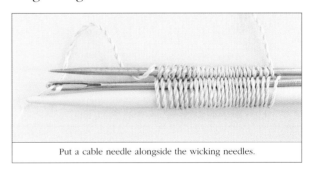

Put a cable needle alongside the wicking needles.

Flower variation.

Figure of Eight with one working end

Sword (Schwertli)

Use the Panicle technique to make this distinctive motif. In the Whole Straw Section you will find a motif with a similar appearance, but it's made very differently.

You will need:

> Schnürli 51cm (20")
> 2 wicking or darning needles
> Needle holder, preferably a cork

Starting

1. The eye of the right-hand needle and the point of the left-hand needle are pushed into the cork and the needles angled so that they taper from 12mm (0.5") apart to a crossing point about 18mm (0.75") above the holder.

Working

1. Work as for a Panicle making eighteen complete stitches. *(Fig. 148)*

Finishing

1. Finish in the same way as the Panicle, shaping the end to a point.

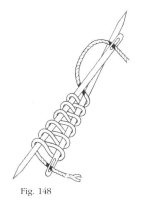

Fig. 148

This star design includes Sword and Horn motifs, see page 135.

Figure of Eight with one working end

Decorative band of horsehair needle lace and Schnürli.

Figure of Eight with one working end

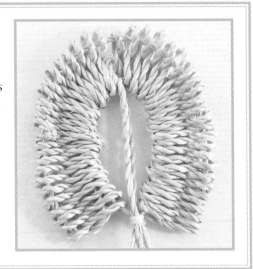

Horseshoe (Hufiseli)

There are several ways to make this motif and vary its finished appearance. First familiarise yourself with the basic method before trying the variations.

You will need:

2 Schnürli 71cm (28")
1 Schnürli 41cm (16")
3 wicking needles
Needle holder
Thread

Starting

1. Thread 5cm (2") of the 41cm (16") Schnürli through the eye of one needle.
2. Put the eye end of threaded needle into the holder, this will be needle 3.
3. Insert the eye end of a second needle into the holder to the left of the threaded needle and just touching, this will be needle 2.
4. Place the third needle 10mm (0.4") to the left of the threaded needle with the eye upwards, this will be needle 1.
(Fig. 149)

Fig. 149

5. Take one of the 71cm (28") Schnürli and hold 5cm (2") in front of the gap between needles 1 and 2.

Working

1. Take the same long end between 1 and 2 to lay behind 3.
2. Wind it around the outside of needle 3 across the front of needle 2 and to the back between 2 and 1.
3. Wind it around the outside of 1 and take it to the back between 1 and 2.
4. Work a total of twenty-two complete moves, working steps 1 to 3. *(Fig. 150)*

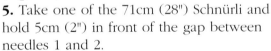

Fig. 150

5. Take the second 71cm length and repeat the working sequence making the same number of stitches.

> **Handy hint**
> *Join new lengths of Schnürli during the working sequence so joins can be positioned in the least conspicuous part of the motif.*

Finishing

1. Check that the Schnürli are damp and then carefully remove the needles from the holder.
2. Pull needle 3 through the stitches leaving at least 5cm (2") of Schnürli at the start of the stitches. Unthread the needle.
3. Rethread the long end through needle 1.
(Fig. 151)
4. Pull the needle through the stitches then unthread. Gently tighten the stitches.
5. Thread the same end through needle 2, then pull through the stitches and tighten gently. *(Fig. 152)*

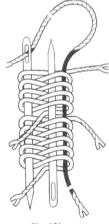

Fig. 151

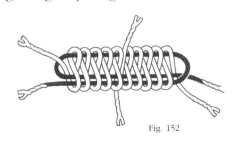

Fig. 152

Figure of Eight with one working end

6. Look at the motif, there are two Schnürli passing through the stitches on one edge and one through the stitches on the other. The side with one thread is the outside of the motif.

7. Feed the two short central ends between the two Schnürli along the inside edge of the motif. One passes from front to back, the other from back to front.

8. Take the two ends of the threaded Schnürli and bend the motif bringing the ends together into the horseshoe shape and then tie together.

9. Trim the ends of the figure of eight windings so that those remaining are the two central and two ends from the threaded Schnürli.

10. Trim the ends.

Add one or more beads to the central Schnürli, or cut them off to create an open centre.

Variation 1

To make a motif that is narrow at each end and wide in the middle make the first set of stitches around needles that are set to widen and the second set around needles set to taper. Use the finishing steps to join the two halves together by threading the single Schnürli through both. Pull needle 3 through the first half, unthread and then re-thread needle 3 of the second half, pull it through. Thread needle 1 then pull it through the second half re-thread needle 1 of the first half and pull it through. Thread needle 2 in the first half, pull through and re-thread into needle 2 of the second half, pull through.

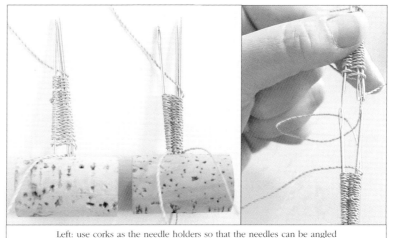

Left: use corks as the needle holders so that the needles can be angled
Right: joining the two halves together.

Variation 2

Follow the Horseshoe instructions, but add an extra needle, numbered 0, to the left of needle 1. Make six figure of eight stitches passing around needles 3, 2 and 1 and the remaining 18 around needles 3, 2 and 0. *(Fig. 153)*

During the final shaping of the motif the stitches must be adjusted to pull them into a gentle curve.

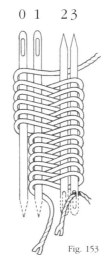

Fig. 153

Tapered Horseshoe variation.

Figure of Eight with two working ends

In this section the length of Schnürli is folded in half and each end is worked alternately. Most of these motifs require a long length of Schnürli so it will be necessary to knot pieces together. Instructions for the Weaver's knot are on page 73.

Small Rosette (Rosettli)

The distance between the two needles is half the diameter of the finished motif. As you work up the needles the stitch tension pulls the needles inward, so fix them into the needle holder so that they taper outwards.

You will need:

>   Schnürli 40cm (16")
>   3 wicking or darning needles
>   Needle holder

Starting

1. Put the points of the needles into the holder 6mm (0.25") apart.

2. Fold the Schnürli in half and put it around the right-hand needle with the two long ends hanging down in front of the holder. If the Schnürli is knotted at its midpoint then start with the knot against the right-hand needle.

3. Take the left-hand end and wind it anti-clockwise over the other and around the right-hand needle to lay at the back of the holder. *(Fig. 154)*

Fig. 154

Working

1. Take the end that is in front of the holder across the front of and then around to the back of the left-hand needle.

2. Bring it to the front between the two needles.

3. Wind it anti-clockwise around the right-hand needle so that it finishes at the front with the long end to the right. *(Fig. 155)*

4. Put this end to the back of the needle holder and hold in place.

5. Bring the unworked end to the front of the holder. It must pass under the end that has just been worked. The two ends must not twist around each other.

6. Repeat the working sequence. *(Fig. 156)*

7. Make a total of 16 stitches leaving at least 5cm (2") of Schnürli for finishing.

> ### Handy hint
> *Aim to produce an even tension while working the stitches. An uneven tension produces an untidy motif.*

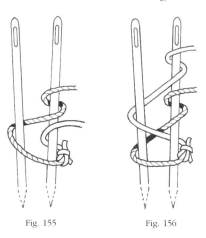

Fig. 155   Fig. 156

Figure of Eight with two working ends

Finishing

1. Thread both ends through the right-hand needle. Put the third needle across the front of the two needles and through the loop. *(Fig. 157)*

2. Pull the threaded needle through the stitches. Unthread the needle.

3. Rethread the ends through the eye of the third needle then pull it through the loops. *(Fig. 158)*

4. Tighten the loops until they almost disappear into the stitches.

5. Shape the stitches into a neat circle.

6. To prevent the two ends coming apart cross the last right-hand loop under the last left-hand loop and thread the ends through. *(Fig. 159)*

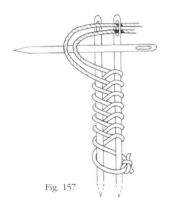

Fig. 157

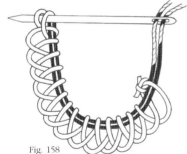

Fig. 158

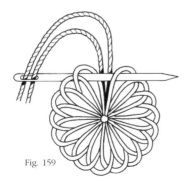

Fig. 159

Variation

Make a half rosette by omitting Finishing steps 5 and 6 and ease the stitches into a semi-circle.

The motifs for this necklace are made from enamelled copper wire.

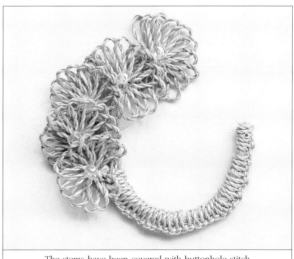

The stems have been covered with buttonhole stitch worked with a Schnürli.

Figure of Eight with two working ends

Three-needle Rose (Rosette)

This time the winding movement begins and ends around the middle needle so although the moves may at first seem strange you are still making a figure of eight movement.

You will need:

Schnürli 110cm (43")
3 wicking needles
Needle holder

Starting

1. Put the points of the needles into the holder 6mm (0.25") apart and placing the left and right-hand needles so they taper outwards. Mentally number the needles 1–3 from left to right.

2. Fold the Schnürli in half and put it around needle 2 with the two long ends hanging down in front of the holder.

3. Take the left-hand end and wind it anti-clockwise in front of the needle 2 and around the needle 3 to lay at the back of the holder. *(Fig. 160)*

Fig. 160

Handy hint

If you cannot remember which thread to use next, do not panic! Look for the last point where the Schnürli passed around needle 2 and is pulled to the left. That was the last complete movement. If necessary unwind to this point. If both ends are at the same point, around needle 2 then pick up the lowest end (that nearest the needle holder) and continue working in sequence.

Working

1. Take the end at the front of the holder and wind it clockwise in front of needle 2 around needle 1 to the back.

2. Bring the end between needles 1 and 2 to the front. Take it across the front of needle 2 then between needles 2 and 3 to the back.

3. Wind the end around needle 3 to the front and the pass it between needles 3 and 2 to the back.

4. Bring the end to the front by passing it between needles 2 and 1. Pull the end to the right, in front of needles 2 and 3 and hold the end at the back of the holder above the one that is already there. *(Fig. 161)*

5. Bring the lower end (not yet worked) to the front, taking care not to twist it around the end that has just been put to the back.

6. Repeat the working sequence. *(Fig. 162)*

7. Make 24 complete stitches leaving 8cm (3") of unused Schnürli for finishing.

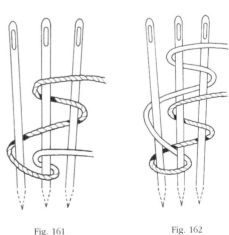

Fig. 161   Fig. 162

Figure of Eight with two working ends

Finishing

1. Thread the top end through needle 3.
Thread the lower end through needle 2.
Take the needles out of the holder.
Remove needle 1 from the stitches. *(Fig. 163)*

2. Pull needles 2 and 3 through the stitches.
Unthread the needles.

3. Pull both ends so the loops tighten against
the end of the stitches.

4. Pass a needle downwards through the row
of stitches previously made around needle 3.

5. Thread both ends in to this needle and pull
through the loops. *(Fig. 164)*

6. Pull on the ends, one at a time and ease
the motif into a flower shape.

7. Arrange the petals and fasten by putting
the last right-hand petal on top of the last
left-hand petal and thread the ends through.
(Fig. 165)

Variations

This motif can also be made as a half flower.

To make longer petals increase the spacing
between needles 1 and 2. To make large
puffy petals replace needle 1 with a cable
needle.

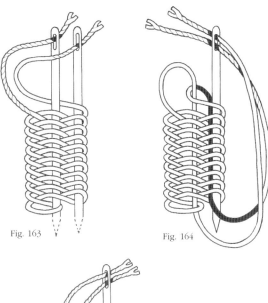

Fig. 163   Fig. 164

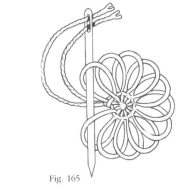

Fig. 165

Variations of the Three-needle Rose.
Beads have been added during making,
and some motifs are made from textile threads.

Figure of Eight with two working ends

Knotted Rosette **(Geknüpfte Rosette)**

Now that you have mastered the Three-needle Rose try this simple variation with a knot worked into alternate stitches.

You will need:

Schnürli 180cm (71")
3 wicking needles
Needle holder

Starting

1. Arrange the needles in the holder so that the distance between needles 1 and 2 is twice that between 2 and 3.
2. Fold the Schnürli so that one end is 15cm (6") longer than the other.
3. Follow the Three-needle Rose instructions keeping the shorter end at the front of the holder as it is the first to be worked.

Working

1. Make one complete figure of eight sequence with the shorter end.
2. Bring the longer end, not yet worked to the front. Make an overhand knot as the Schnürli passes around needle 1. *(Fig. 167 and inset Fig. 166)*

Finishing

1. Use the Three-needle Rose method.

Variation

This needle arrangement makes the knots more prominent. Add an extra needle to the left-hand side of the holder, spacing it about 6mm (0.25") to the left of needle 1. Follow the instructions for the Knotted Rosette making plain stitches around the extra needle and knotted stitches around needle 1. *(Fig. 169)*

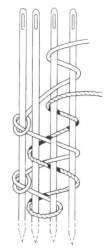

Fig. 169

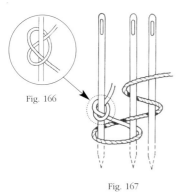

Fig. 166

Fig. 167

3. Complete the move and take the end to the back. *(Fig. 168)*
4. Continue the working sequence and make a total of 24 stitches finishing with a knotted stitch. Leave 8cm (3") of unworked Schnürli for finishing.

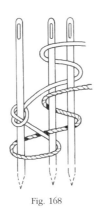

Fig. 168

Knotted Rose variation.

Figure of Eight with two working ends

Square Rosette

Swiss workers used a special tool to make this simple motif. The Schnürli is worked around a zig-zag arrangement of pins set into a narrow board.

You will need:

    Schnürli 250cm (98")
    Tool fitted with 2 needles approx. 15cm (6")
    1 extra needle

Starting

1. Fold the Schnürli in half and loop over needle 1. Take the left-hand end in front of needle 2 and then to the back of the holder.

Working

1. Take the end at the front of the holder and hook it over the first pin. Bring it to the right in front of needle 1, behind and then around needle 2 to the front. Take it behind and around needle 1 to the front. Hold it at the back of the holder. (*Fig. 170*)

2. Bring the unused end to the front and hook it over the next pin; repeat the figure of eight move. (*Fig. 171*)

3. Repeat the working sequence until all the pins have been worked.

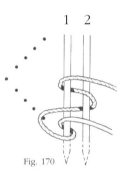

Fig. 170

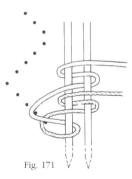

Fig. 171

Finishing

1. Follow the instructions for the Three-needle Rose, carefully lifting the stitches off the pins after the two needles are threaded. (*Fig. 172*)

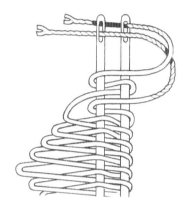

Fig. 172

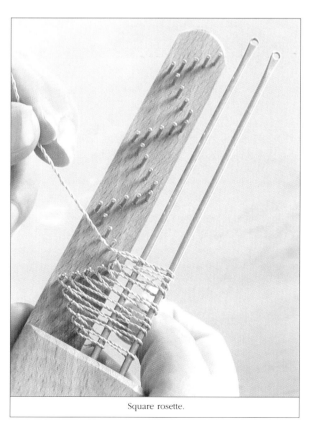

Square rosette.

Complex Rosettes

Now you can begin to make large motifs that are ideal for centrepieces. In the past these were used to make the centre of bonnet crowns. These rosettes are easy to make but don't attempt them until you are familiar with making the basic components of each.

Three-needle Rose with a Needle Rose edge
(Rosette mit Nadelröslirand)

The Three-needle Rose is worked around needles 2, 3 and 4.
The Needle Rose is worked around needles 1 and 2.
The Rosette is linked on needle 2.

You will need:

> Schnürli 130cm (51") for the Three-needle Rose
> Schnürli 120cm (47") for the Needle Rose
> 4 wicking needles
> Needle holder

Starting

1. Fix needles 2, 3 and 4, 6mm (0.25") apart in the holder. Fix needle 1, 12mm (0.5") to the left of needle 2.
2. Follow the Three-needle Rose instructions setting up the 130cm (51") length around needle 3.
3. Fold the Schnürli for the Needle Rose 15cm (6") from one end and set up the 120cm (47") length around needle 2. (*Fig. 173*)

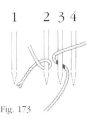

Fig. 173

Working

1. Make one figure of eight stitch for the Three-needle Rose and put the end to the back of the holder.
2. Make one half hitch for the Needle Rose and hold the end against the front of the holder.
3. Using the unworked end make the next figure of eight stitch for the Three-needle Rose.
4. Make the first loop and half hitch for the Needle Rose. (*Fig. 174*)

Fig. 174

5. Continue the working sequence until there are 18 completed loops around needle 1. Leave 15cm (6") of each end for finishing.

Finishing

1. Thread the ends of the Three-needle Rose into the needles 3 and 4.
2. Thread the end from the Needle Rose through needle 2 putting a needle through the loop for the final finishing.
3. Remove the needles from the holder and remove needle 1.
4. Pull the remaining three needles through the stitches.
5. Finish the Three-needle Rose.
6. Finish the Needle Rose.
7. The ends from the Three-needle Rose can be threaded back through the stitches and the surplus cut off. The ends from the Needle Rose can be threaded back through the half hitches and the surplus cut off.

Variation

Once you feel confident work the Needle Rose with two Schnürli. You can also add a Needle Rose edge to a Two-needle Rose (Small Rosette).

Three-needle Rose with two Schnürli worked as the Needle Rose.

Complex Rosettes

Rosette with a Two-needle Rose centre

The Two-needle Rose is worked around needles 3 and 4, the Three-needle Rose around 1, 2 and 3. The Rosette is linked on needle 3.

You will need:

Schnürli, 120cm (47") for the Two-needle Rose
Schnürli 180cm (71") for the Three-needle Rose
4 wicking needles
Needle holder

Starting

1. Fix needles 2, 3 and 4, 6mm (0.25") apart in the holder. Fix needle 1, 12mm (0.5") to the left of needle 2.
2. Put the 120cm (47") length around needle 4 and the 180cm (71") length around needle 2 and arrange the ends ready to begin the working sequence. (*Fig. 175*)

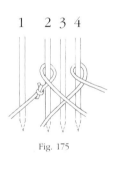

Fig. 175

Fig. 176

Working

1. Make one stitch of the Two-needle Rose.
2. Make one stitch of the Three-needle Rose. (*Fig. 176*)
3. Take the unworked end of the Two-needle Rose and make one stitch.
4. Take the unworked end of the Three-needle Rose and make one stitch.
5. Work 28 stitches ending with one stitch of the Two-needle Rose. Leave 15cm (6") of each end for finishing.

Finishing

1. Thread both ends of the Two-needle Rose through needle 4.
2. Thread the ends of the Three-needle Rose through needles 2 and 3. (*Fig. 177*)
3. Remove the needles from the holder.
4. Remove needle 1.
5. Finish the Three-needle Rose but do not pull into a circle until the centre has been finished.
6. Completely finish the Two-needle Rose.
7. Finish the Three-needle Rose.
8. Thread the unworked ends back through the stitches and cut off the surplus.

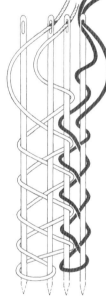

Fig. 177

To show how this complex Rosette interlaces, the centre is made from dyed Schnürli.

Complex Rosettes

Rosette with a Three-needle Rose centre

The Three-needle Rose is worked around needles 2, 3 and 4.
The Two-needle Rose is worked around needles 1 and 2.
The Rosette is linked on needle 2.

You will need:

Schnürli 130cm (51") for the Three-needle Rose
Schnürli 170cm (70") for the Two-needle Rose
4 wicking needles
Needle holder

Starting

1. Fix needles 2, 3 and 4, 6mm (0.25") apart in the holder. Fix needle 1, 12mm (0.5") to the left of needle 2.
2. Loop the 130cm (51") length around needle 3. Loop the 170cm (70") length around needle 2 and arrange the ends ready to begin working. *(Fig. 178)*

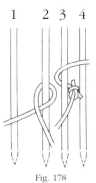

Fig. 178

Working

1. Work one stitch of the Three-needle Rose.
2. Work one stitch of the Two-needle Rose.
3. Make 28 stitches ending with a stitch of the Three-needle Rose. Leave 15cm (6") of each end for finishing. *(Fig. 179)*

Fig. 179

Finishing

1. Thread the ends of the Three-needle Rose through needles 3 and 4.
2. Thread both ends of the Two-needle Rose through needle 2. *(Fig. 180)*
3. Finish the Three-needle Rose.
4. Finish the Two-needle Rose.
5. Thread the unworked ends back through the stitches and cut off the surplus.

Fig. 180

> ***Handy hint***
> *Take care not to over-tighten the outer ring of stitches. They must be allowed to spread out without bunching.*

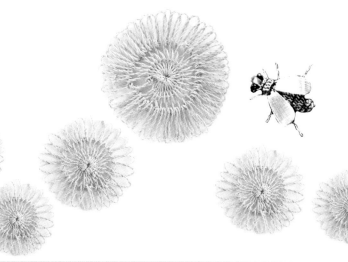

Complex Rosettes

Double Edge Rosette with a Three-needle centre

This time two stitches of the Two-needle Rose are worked between each single stitch of the Three-needle Rose.

You will need:

Schnürli 130cm (51") for the Three-needle Rose
Schnürli 200cm (79") for the Two-needle Rose
4 wicking needles
Needle holder

Starting

1. Follow the instructions for a Rosette with a Three-needle Rose centre.

Working

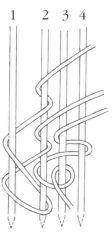

Fig. 181

1. Make one figure of eight stitch for the Three-needle Rose.
2. Make two figure of eight stitches for the Two-needle Rose. *(Fig. 181)*
3. Make 28 stitches, counted around needle 4, ending with a stitch of the Three-needle Rose and leaving 15cm (6") for finishing.

Finishing

1. Follow the instructions for the Rosette with a Three-needle Rose centre.

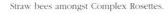

Straw bees amongst Complex Rosettes.

Complex Rosettes

Five-needle Rosette

For this motif needle 1 is a cable needle. The centre of the Rosette is worked around needles 3, 4 and 5 and the edge is worked around needles 1, 2 and 3. The Rosette is linked around needle 3.

You will need:

Schnürli 130cm (51") for the centre Rose
Schnürli 300cm (118") for the outer Rose
4 wicking needles
Cable needle
Needle holder

Starting

1. Attach the cable needle to the left-hand side of the holder, this is needle 1. Leave a 12mm (0.5") gap between needles 1 and 2 and 6mm (0.25") gaps between needles 2, 3, 4 and 5.
2. Put the 130cm (51") length around needle 4 and the 300cm (118") length around needle 2. Arrange the ends ready to begin working.

Working

1. Start by making one figure of eight stitch around needles 3, 4 and 5.
2. Make two figure of eight stitches around needles 1, 2 and 3. *(Fig. 182)*
3. Work 24 stitches, counted around needle 5, finish with a stitch around needles 3, 4 and 5.
4. Leave 15cm (6") for finishing the central rose and 30cm (12") for finishing the outer one.

Fig. 182

> ### *Handy hint*
> *Join new lengths during the last few stitches of the working sequence to ensure that there are sufficiently long ends for finishing.*

Finishing

1. Thread the ends that form the centre of the rosette through needles 4 and 5.
2. Thread the ends that form the edge through needles 2 and 3. *(Fig. 183)*
3. Pull needles 1, 4 and 5 through the stitches.
4. Finish the central Three-needle Rose, but do not pull it into a circle.
5. Finish the outer Three-needle Rose. The needle is re-inserted through the double row of stitches worked around needle 3. Do not pull into a circle.
6. Pull the centre into a circle and thread the unworked ends back through the stitches.
7. Pull the edge into a circle. Arrange the stitches taking care not to over-tighten.
8. Thread the unworked ends back through the stitches.
9. Make the final arrangement of the stitches and then cut off the surplus ends.

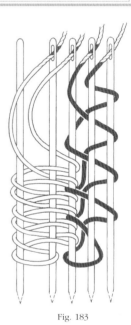

Fig. 183

Decorative Edgings around a Form

MAKING TEMPLATES FOR DECORATIVE EDGINGS

Mark the template onto a thin card and cover with clear non-reflective self-adhesive plastic. Use the following calculation to make a template for a ready-made wheel.

1. Measure the circumference of the wheel. Or multiply the diameter by 3.14 (π) to find the circumference.
2. Divide the circumference of the wheel by the size of pattern repeat.
3. This gives you the number of complete repeats needed for one complete rotation. If the calculation produces a fractional number of pattern repeats use the following calculation to adjust the size of pattern repeat.
4. Divide the circumference of the wheel by the number of pattern repeats required for one complete rotation. This calculation will give you the size of pattern repeat.

Example

Wheel circumference 300mm (<12"), diameter 95.5mm (3.75").
Number of pattern repeats for one complete rotation 25. Pattern repeat 12mm (<0.5").
When using knotting boards first measure the board length and then divide by the size of pattern repeat. The templates must be drawn to ensure the pattern continues on to the second block without error.

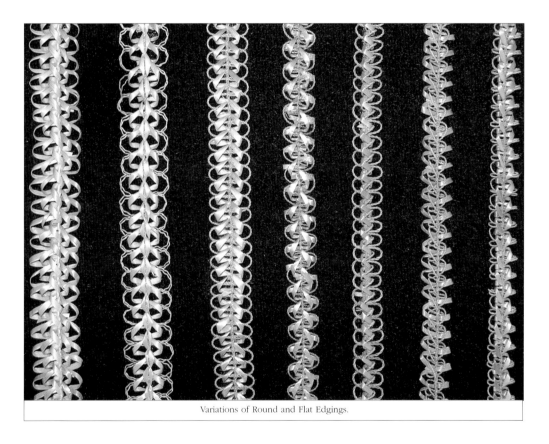

Variations of Round and Flat Edgings.

Decorative Edgings around a Form

Edgings made around forms were a speciality of the village of Villmergen where the work was known as Stiefelring (little boot plait). The name may have been derived from the shaped ends of the wooden sticks used by the workers.

Edging with small loop (Bögli)

The central locking stitches are made using Schnürli, but you can use thread or splints. The diameter of needle will affect the size of loop and the spacing of the needles affects the final width.

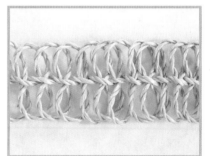

You will need:
>   2 long needles, mattress or cable
>   Needle holder
>   4 lengths of Schnürli
>   Thread

Starting

1. Put the needles into the holder, points downwards, 1cm (0.75") apart. Mentally number the needles 1 (left) and 2 (right).
2. Using thread tie the four Schnürli together at one end.
3. Position two Schnürli at 12 and 6 o'clock, these will make the central locking stitches.
4. Position two behind the needles at 9 and 3 o'clock. *(Fig. 184)*

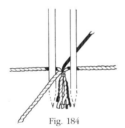

Fig. 184

Working

1. Start with the left-hand Schnürli, twist it from behind needle 1, around the outside of that needle to the front and then between the needles to the back, resting it behind needle 2. *(Fig. 185)*
2. Twist the right-hand Schnürli from behind needle 2, around the outside of that needle to the front and then between the needles to the back, resting it behind needle 1. *(Fig. 186)*
3. The next two moves lock the loops in place. Take the 6 o'clock Schnürli between the needles passing diagonally to the right over the crossed loops. *(Fig. 187)*
4. Bring the 12 o'clock Schnürli from the back to the front passing it diagonally to the left of the other locking Schnürli. *(Fig. 188)*
5. Continue the working sequence until the required length has been made. Remove the needles from the holder when the edging is long enough to hold them. As work progresses, the edging can slide off the end of the needles.

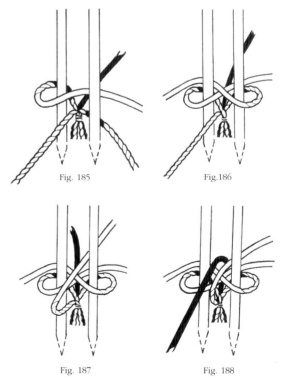

Fig. 185

Fig.186

Fig. 187

Fig. 188

Decorative Edgings around a Form

Joining

1. Join on to the lengths of Schnürli as necessary by using a Weaver's knot, page 73. Keep the knots in the centre of the work where they will be less visible.

Finishing

1. Finish by tying the ends together with thread.

Variation

Make the loops by using splints instead of Schnürli. To join new splints overlap the old and new ends under the locking stitches.

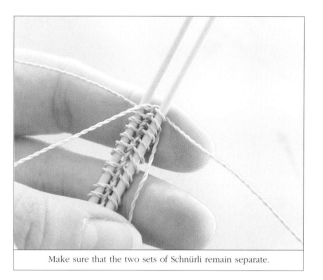

Make sure that the two sets of Schnürli remain separate.

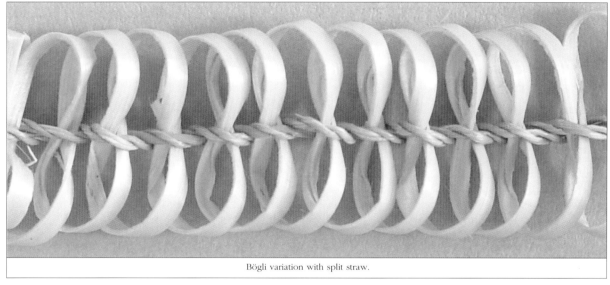

Bögli variation with split straw.

These lengths of Bögli have been worked into a three-end Schnürli plait.

Decorative Edgings around a Form

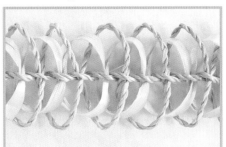

Round and Flat Edging (Flader Ring)

This edging combines splints and Schnürli, which are worked around four needles thus creating loops of different sizes.

You will need:

> 4 lengths Schnürli
> 2 splints
> 2 mattress needles
> 2 cable needles
> Needle holder
> Thread

Starting

1. Put the cable needles in the holder about 5mm (0.25") apart. Put the mattress needles 5mm (0.25") outside the first pair. Mentally number the needles 1 to 4 from left to right.
2. Follow the instructions for the previous edging putting one Schnürli and one splint at both 9 o'clock and 3 o'clock. *(Fig. 189)*

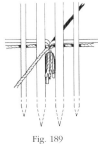

Fig. 189

Working

1. First work the left-hand Schnürli around needle 1. *(Fig. 190)*
2. Work the right-hand Schnürli around needle 4. *(Fig. 191)*
3. Lock the Schnürli in place Pass the 6 o'clock Schnürli between needles 2 and 3 passing diagonally to the right over the crossed loops. Bring the 12 o'clock Schnürli from the back to the front passing it diagonally to the left of the other locking Schnürli. *(Fig. 192)*
4. Take the left-hand splints around needle 2, and the right-hand splint around needle 3. Twist the splint so that the shiny side is outwards *(Fig. 193)*
5. Lock the splint loops in place using the sequence in step 3.
6. Continue the working sequence until the required length has been made.

Joining

1. Use a Weaver's knot, page 73, to join the Schnürli. Join the splints by overlapping the old and new ends using the Schnürli locking stitch to hold in place.

Finishing

1. Finish by tying the ends together with thread.

> *Handy hint*
> To prevent confusion between the two locking stitch Schnürli and the loop stitch Schnürli mark the ends of one pair.

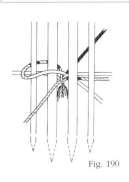

Fig. 190

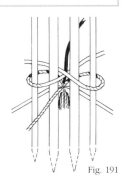

Fig. 191

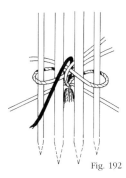

Fig. 192

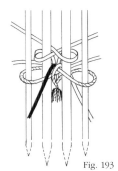

Fig. 193

Decorative Edgings around a Form

This 19th century bonnet is made from horsehair and straw.

Decorative Edgings around a Passive

Although these can be worked in-hand they will be neater if you work on a knotting wheel or board using a pattern template. The passive can be any type of thread or wire.

Zig-zag with loop on one edge (Schnürli-Zaggli)

This plait can also be made with splints or whole straw in which case the final result will have a very different appearance.

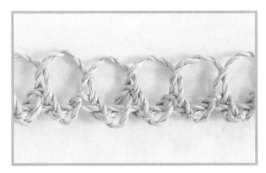

You will need:

> Passive thread
> 3 lengths of Schnürli
> Knotting wheel or board
> Template
> Pins
> Thread

Starting

1. Use a template with a vertical lines spaced 5mm (0.25") apart and the horizontals spaced at 5mm (0.25").
2. Tie together the three lengths of Schnürli and the passive.
3. Pin both ends of the passive to the left-hand vertical line so that it is taut whilst work progresses.
4. Position the three Schnürli to the right of the passive, with one lying horizontally and two vertically.
5. Take the right-hand vertical Schnürli over the second vertical and then under the passive to lay horizontally to the left of the passive. (*Fig. 194*)

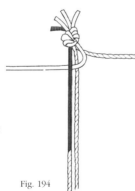

Fig. 194

> ### Handy hint
> *Begin working with three Schnürli of different lengths so joins are staggered throughout the work.*

Working

1. Bring the remaining right-hand vertical Schnürli over the passive to lay below the horizontal Schnürli on the left. (*Fig. 195*)
2. Bring the top left-hand horizontal Schnürli downwards over the second end to lay parallel to the passive. Then take it behind the passive to lay horizontally on the right.
3. Bring the remaining left-hand Schnürli over the passive. (*Fig. 196*)
4. There are three horizontal Schnürli on the right. Bring the middle Schnürli down to lay parallel to the right of the passive. (*Fig. 197*)
5. Take the top Schnürli under the right-hand horizontal, over the right-hand vertical Schnürli and under the passive. Lay it horizontally to the left of the passive. The remaining right-hand horizontal Schnürli forms the next loop. (*Fig. 198*)
6. Continue the working sequence until the required length has been made. To achieve a regular pattern the loops can be pinned in position once made.

Decorative Edgings around a Passive

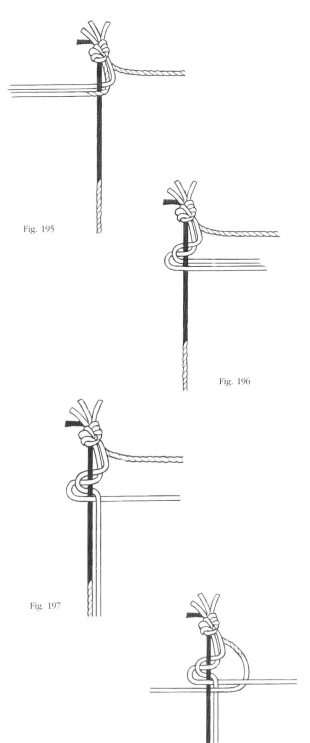

Fig. 195

Fig. 196

Fig. 197

Fig. 198

Joining

1. Join new lengths of Schnürli using a Weaver's knot, page 73. Keep the knots in the centre of the work where they will be less visible.

Finishing

1. Tie the ends together. Once dry, the tie can be removed.

Variation

This edging can be worked with a double Schnürli passive and three pairs of Schnürli.

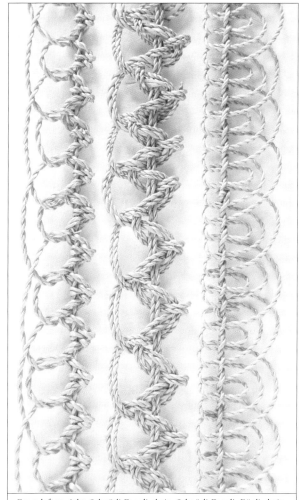

From left to right: Schnürli-Zaggli chain, Schnürli-Zaggli, Bögli chain.

Decorative Edgings around a Passive

Zig-Zag with loop on both edges (Schnürli Gimpli)

By adding one more working Schnürli you can work a loop along each edge.

You will need:
- Passive thread
- 4 lengths of Schnürli
- Knotting wheel or board
- Template
- Pins

Starting

1. Use a template with three vertical lines spaced 5mm (0.25") apart and the horizontals also spaced at 5mm (0.25").

2. Arrange one Schnürli horizontally to the left of the passive, one to the right of the passive and two vertically to the right of the passive.

3. Take the right-hand Schnürli of the two verticals and bring it over the next vertical and under the passive, to lay horizontally on the left. Bring the remaining vertical Schnürli over the passive to lay horizontally below the Schnürli on the left. *(Fig. 199)*

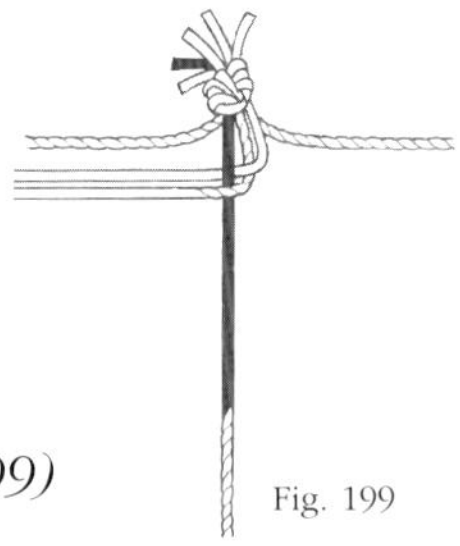

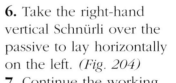

Fig. 199

Working

1. There are three horizontal Schnürli on the left. Bring the middle one down over the lowest horizontal Schnürli to lay parallel to the left of the passive. *(Fig. 200)*

2. Bring the top left-hand horizontal Schnürli under the remaining horizontal Schnürli, over the left-hand vertical and under the passive to lay horizontally to the right. Pin the loop in place, optional.

3. Bring the left-hand vertical over the passive to lay horizontally on the right. *(Fig. 201)*

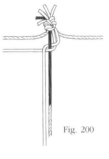

Fig. 200

Fig. 201

4. Fold the middle Schnürli downwards over the lower horizontal to lay parallel to the right of the passive. *(Fig. 202)*

5. Make the right-hand loop. Bring the top Schnürli under the horizontal Schnürli, over the right-hand vertical, under the passive and lay it horizontally to the left. Pin the loop in place, optional. *(Fig. 203)*

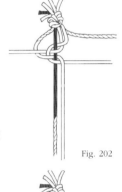

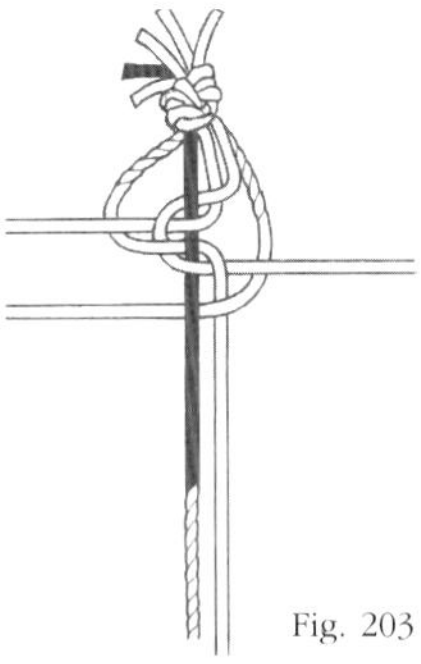

Fig. 202

Fig. 203

6. Take the right-hand vertical Schnürli over the passive to lay horizontally on the left. *(Fig. 204)*

7. Continue the working sequence until the required length has been made.

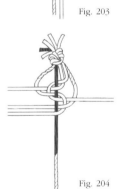

Fig. 204

> **Handy hint**
> *Keep the Schnürli damp as you work.*

Decorative Edgings around a Passive

Joining

1. Follow the previous instructions.

Finishing

1. Follow the previous instructions.

Variation

This edging can be worked with pairs of Schnürli around either a single or double Schnürli passive.

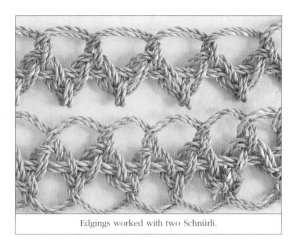

Edgings worked with two Schnürli.

Elaborate edgings and Schnürli are worked through Ring plaits.

Decorative Edgings around a Passive

Schnürli Cord with loop on one edge

The loop on the edge of this cord is unstable until locked in place by the next set of moves so it is important to pin each one in place.

You will need:
>   Passive thread
>   3 lengths of Schnürli
>   Knotting wheel or board
>   Template
>   Pins

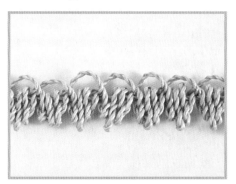

Starting

1. Make a template with the three vertical lines spaced 5mm (0.25") apart and the horizontal lines at 5mm (0.25").
2. Tie together the passive and three lengths of Schnürli. Pin to the template. Secure the passive to the central vertical line.
3. Place two Schnürli to the right, one vertical and the other horizontal, and one to the left of the passive at an angle not less than 30°. *(Fig. 205)*
4. Take the right-hand vertical Schnürli and bring it to the left, passing over the passive and under the 30° Schnürli.

Fig. 205

Working

1. Work the same end back over the 30° Schnürli, then under the passive. Make three figure of eight stitches finishing with the end laying horizontally to the right.
2. Take the remaining left-hand Schnürli over the passive to lay horizontally on the right. *(Fig. 206)*

Fig. 206

3. Bring the top horizontal Schnürli down, over the other two and under the passive so that it lays on the left at an angle of about 30°. Pin the loop, optional. *(Fig. 207)*
4. There are two Schnürli on the right. Take the top horizontal Schnürli over the second and then over the passive to the left-hand side, then under the left-hand Schnürli. *(Fig. 208)*
5. Pull the end.
6. Continue the working sequence until the required length has been made.

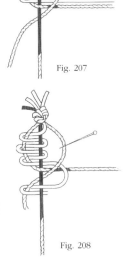

Fig. 207

Fig. 208

Joining

1. Follow the previous instructions.

Finishing

1. Follow the previous instructions.

> **Handy hint**
> *The moves may be easier to make if you use a needle.*

Decorative Edgings around a Passive

Schnürli Cord with loop on both edges

Add an extra Schnürli to make a cord with a loop on each edge.

You will need:
> Passive thread
> 4 lengths of Schnürli
> Knotting wheel or boards
> Template
> Pins

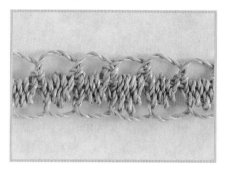

Starting

1. Position one Schnürli horizontally to the right and one to the left of the passive.
2. Place one Schnürli vertically to the right of the passive and the last Schnürli at an angle not less than 30° to the left of the passive.

Working

1. Take the right-hand vertical over the passive and under the 30° Schnürli.
2. Make 3½ figure of eight stitches around the 30° Schnürli finishing with the working end passing over the passive and under the diagonal Schnürli.
3. Move the 30° Schnürli to lay parallel to the passive. *(Fig. 209)*
4. Bring down the top left-hand horizontal Schnürli passing under the remaining horizontal. Pull it to the right over the left-hand vertical and under the passive. Pin the loop in place. *(Fig. 210)*
5. Bring the left-hand vertical to the right by passing it over the passive. *(Fig. 211)*
6. There are three horizontal Schnürli on the right. Bring the middle one down so that it lays vertically to the right of the passive. *(Fig. 212)*
7. Form the right-hand loop by bringing the top horizontal Schnürli down. Pass it under the horizontal, over the right-hand vertical and under the passive. Lay it at an angle of 30° to the left of the passive. Pin in place. *(Fig. 213)*
8. Continue the working sequence until the required length has been made. *(Fig. 214)*

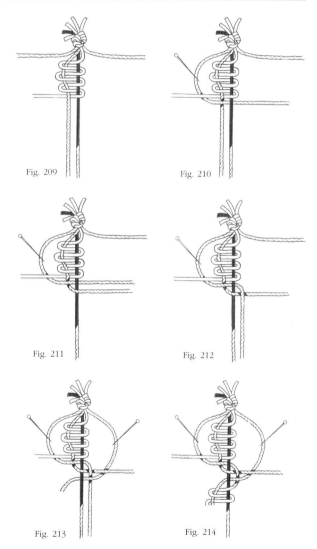

Fig. 209

Fig. 210

Fig. 211

Fig. 212

Fig. 213

Fig. 214

Joining

1. Follow the previous instructions.

Finishing

1. Follow the previous instructions.

Macramé (Gestrick)

Attractive Macramé depends upon accuracy, so be precise with the spacing and alignment of knots.

Narrow Square Knot Edging

You can alter the appearance of this edging by varying the spacing of the knots, but whatever spacing you choose, do keep them even.

You will need:

    4 lengths of Schnürli
    Knotting wheel or board
    Template
    Pins

Starting

1. Use a template with the three vertical lines spaced 5mm (0.25") apart and the horizontal lines at 10mm (0.5").
2. Tie together four lengths of Schnürli and pin to the central vertical line.
3. Mentally number the Schnürli 1 to 4 from left to right.
4. Arrange Schnürli 2 and 3 in the centre with Schnürli 1 to the left and Schnürli 4 to the right. *(Fig. 215)*

1 2 3 4

Fig. 215

SQUARE KNOT

This square knot is made around passives and consists of two half knots, one left and one right.

a

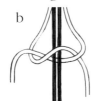
b

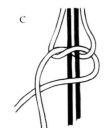
c

d

Working

1. Using Schnürli 3 make a half hitch around Schnürli 4 by taking the passive across the front of 4 then around so that it passes over the start of the loop. Put Schnürli 3 back into its starting position. Pin the loop in place.

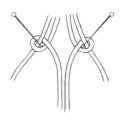

Fig. 216

2. Using Schnürli 2 make a mirror image half hitch around Schnürli 1. Pin the loop in place. *(Fig. 216)*
3. Take Schnürli 1 and 4 and make the first part of the square knot. Place a pin immediately below the knot. *(Fig. 217)*

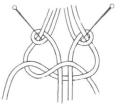

Fig. 217

4. Make the second half of the knot with Schnürli 1 and 4. Tighten the knot and straighten Schnürli 2 and 3 taking care not to distort the pattern. *(Fig. 218)*
5. Continue the working sequence until you have the required length.

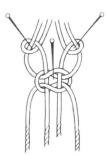

Fig. 218

Macramé (Gestrick)

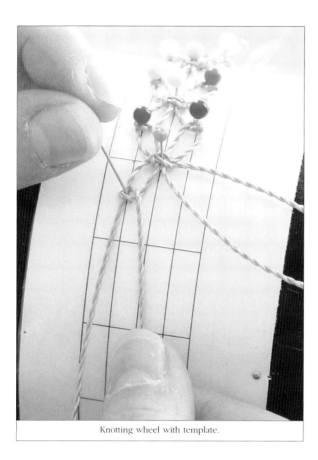

Knotting wheel with template.

Joining

1. Use a Weaver's knot, page 73, and keep the joins in the centre of the work where they will be less conspicuous.

Finishing

1. Tie the ends together. This tie can be removed once the Schnürli are dry.

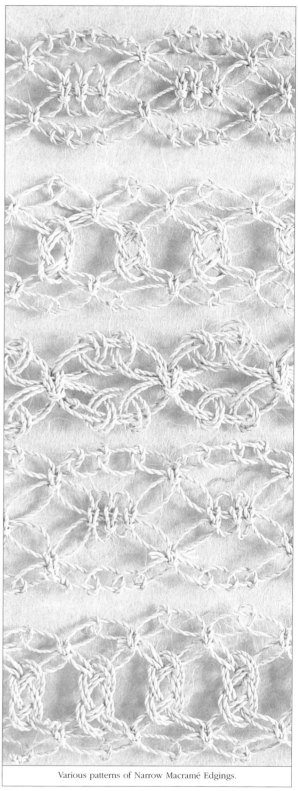

Various patterns of Narrow Macramé Edgings.

Macramé (Gestrick)

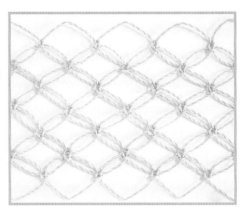

Wide Square Knot Edging

This popular product was made in a variety of widths, up to 50cm (20") wide. The pattern sequence comprises two rows. Row A has three square knots across the width. Row B has four knots.

You will need:

> 14 lengths of Schnürli
> Knotting wheel or board
> Template
> Pins

Starting

1. Make a template with nine vertical lines spaced 15mm (0.5") apart and the horizontal lines at 10mm (0.375").
2. Divide and tie the Schnürli into two groups of four and two groups of three.
3. Pin them to the board, 15mm (0.5") apart, in the following order, from left to right: three, four, four, and three.
4. Mentally number the ends from left, 1 to right, 14.

Working

Row A
1. Schnürli 1 is not used in this row.
2. Make the first working group with Schnürli 2, 3, 4 and 5.
3. Use Schnürli 2 and 5 to make a square knot around Schnürli 3 and 4. Pin the knot.
4. Make the second working group from Schnürli 6, 7, 8 and 9.
5. Use Schnürli 6 and 9 to make a square knot around 7 and 8. Pin the knot.
6. Make the third working group from Schnürli 10, 11, 12 and 13.
7. Use Schnürli 10 and 13 to make a square knot around 11 and 12. Pin the knot.
8. Schnürli 14 is not used in this row.
Row B
9. Insert a pin into the template 15mm to the left of the first knot in row A. Put Schnürli 1 outside the pin.
10. Use Schnürli 1 and 3 to make a square knot around Schnürli 2.

11. Use Schnürli 4 and 7 to make square knot around Schnürli 5 and 6. Pin the knot.
12. Use Schnürli 8 and 11 to make a square knot around Schnürli 9 and 10. Pin the knot.
13. Insert a pin into the template 15mm to the right of the last knot in row A. Put Schnürli 14 outside the pin.
14. Use Schnürli 12 and 14 to make a square knot around Schnürli 13. Pin the knot. *(Fig. 219)*
15. Continue the working sequence until you have made the required length.

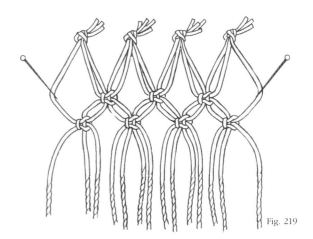

Fig. 219

Handy hint
Use pins to control the spacing of the knots and to keep the passives parallel as work progresses.

Macramé (Gestrick)

Joining

1. Stagger the joins and try to keep them close to the knots so that they are less visible.

Finishing

1. End with a row of four knots. When dry trim the ends close to the knots.

Variation

Widen the edging by adding extra groups of four Schnürli to the centre. Narrow the pattern by leaving out one group of four.

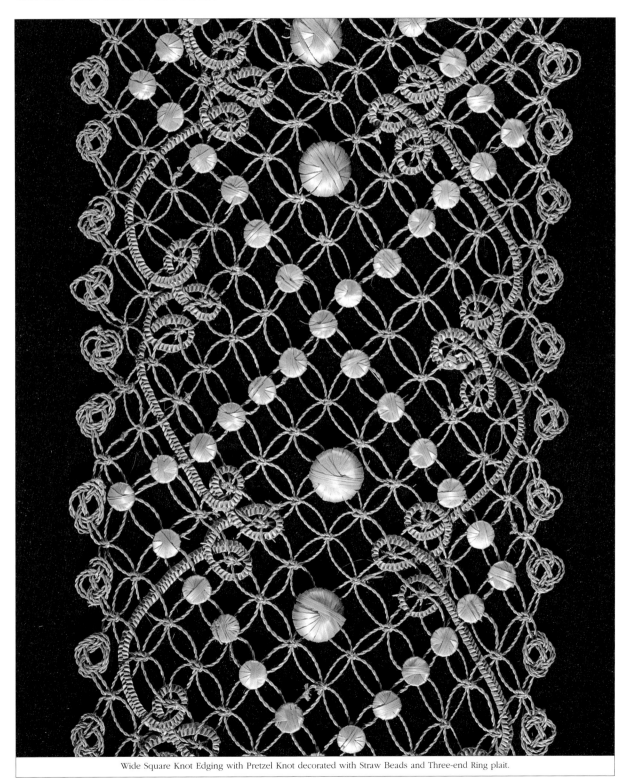

Wide Square Knot Edging with Pretzel Knot decorated with Straw Beads and Three-end Ring plait.

Macramé (Gestrick)

Wide Square Knot Edging with Pretzel Knot

This decorative edge can be added to a pattern of any width by adding two extra Schnürli to one edge. The knot can be added to both edges, but remember to add extra Schnürli.

You will need:

    13 lengths of Schnürli
    Knotting wheel or board
    Template
    Pins
    Form, cable needle

Starting

1. Use a template with vertical lines spaced 15mm (0.5") apart and the horizontals 10mm (0.375").
2. Divide and tie the Schnürli into two groups of four, one group of two and one group of three.
3. Pin them to the board, 15mm (0.5") apart, in the following order, from left to right: three, four, four, and two.
4. Mentally number the ends from left, 1, to right, 13.

PRETZEL KNOT

Associated with decorative braids this knot provides an attractive edge.
To create evenly sized knots use a form.

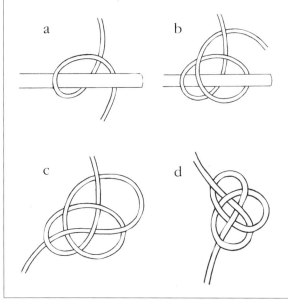

Working

Row A

1. Schnürli 1 is not worked in this row.
2. Make the first working group with Schnürli 2, 3, 4 and 5.
3. Use Schnürli 2 and 5 to make a square knot around Schnürli 3 and 4. Pin the knot.
4. Make the second working group from Schnürli 6, 7, 8 and 9.
5. Use Schnürli 6 and 9 to make a square knot around 7 and 8. Pin the knot.
6. Make the third working group from Schnürli 10, 11, 12 and 13.
7. Use Schnürli 10 and 13 to make a square knot around Schnürli 11 and 12. Pin the knot.

Row B

8. Insert a pin into the template 15mm to the left of the first knot in row A. Put Schnürli 1 outside the pin.
9. Use Schnürli 1 and 3 to make a square knot around Schnürli 2.
10. Use Schnürli 4 and 7 to make square knot around Schnürli 5 and 6. Pin the knot.
11. Use Schnürli 8 and 11 to make a square knot around Schnürli 9 and 10. Pin the knot.
12. Use Schnürli 12 and 13 to make the Pretzel Knot. *(Fig. 220)*
13. Pin the Pretzel Knot in place 15mm (0.5") to the right of the last square knot.
14. Continue the working sequence until the required length is made.

Macramé (Gestrick)

Joining

1. Follow the Square Knot Edging method.

Finishing

1. Follow the Square Knot Edging method.

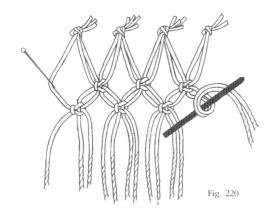

Fig. 220

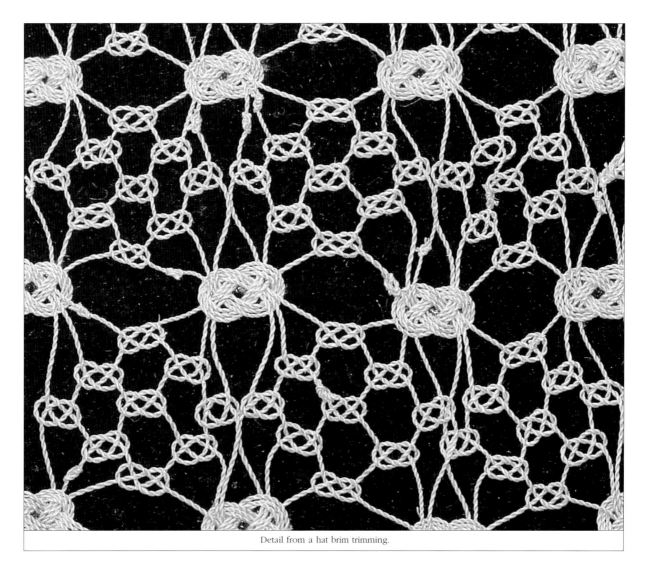

Detail from a hat brim trimming.

Needle Lace

This technique was used to make hats and a bag to accompany the regional costume of the women of the Freiamt.

Doily

The stitches radiate from a central boss which can be a sewn circle of plait, an arrangement of Spreuer, or a combination of split straw and Schnürli motifs arranged into a circular pattern. Any of the Complex Rosettes are particularly suitable.

You will need:
    A central boss
    Schnürli
    Darning or crewel needle
    Pin board
    Pins

Starting

1. Pin the boss to the centre of the pin board.
2. Tie one end of the first Schnürli to the central boss.
3. Work a foundation row of single Brussels stitch spacing them equidistant around the boss and keeping the loops the same size. As you work take care not to unwind the ply of the Schnürli. *(Fig. 221)*

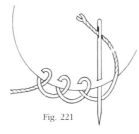

Fig. 221

Working

1. When you arrive back at the first stitch of the previous row make a loop that is larger than the previous ones.
2. Make a double Brussels stitch around the first loop of the previous row. Gently tighten the stitches before making the next loop and stitches. *(Fig. 222)*

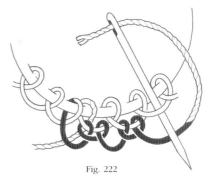

Fig. 222

3. Pin the loops in place as you work.
4. Increase the loop size on each subsequent row to ensure that the doily lays flat.
5. Continue until the doily is the required size.

> **Handy hint**
> *Mount the pin board on to a lazy Susan or cake-icing turntable.*

Needle Lace

Joining

1. Use a Weaver's knot, page 73, positioning it on the loop so that it is covered by the next row of stitches. *(Fig. 223)*

2. Joins made on the last row of the doily should be positioned within the Brussels stitch.

Fig. 223

Finishing

1. The loops of the final row must maintain the circular effect. Finish at the end of a complete circuit making the final loop smaller so that it lays level with the first loop of the final row.

2. Use an overhand knot to fasten the end to the loop.

3. Trim the end.

4. The edge can be left as plain loops or work a Pretzel Knot, page 118, between each loop linking to each loop with either a single or double Brussels stitch.

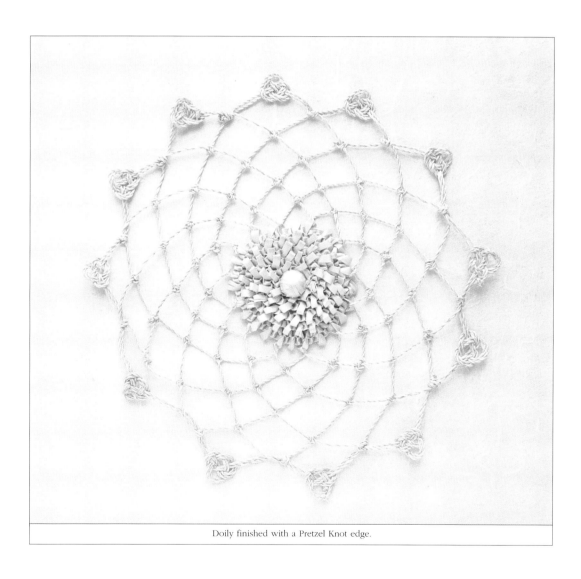

Doily finished with a Pretzel Knot edge.

Wheel Plait (Rädligeflecht)

Manufacture of this product began in the 1840s and is attributed to a family in the Fricktal, Switzerland. There were various patterns and sometimes one or more of the Schnürli were replaced with other types of thread, plait, or split straw. The finished mesh can be decorated with split straw, motifs or plait.

Seven-end mesh

The diagrams show a wheel with the pins configured in a scalloped pattern along one edge. This edge is known as the head whilst the left-hand edge is the foot. The centre of the work is the body.

You will need:
- Schnürli
- Rädli wheel
- Sticky tape, optional

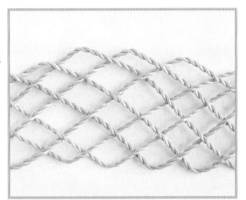

Starting

1. Take six Schnürli and using a Weaver's knot, page 73, make three pairs.

2. Starting at any part of the pin pattern lay one pair of Schnürli horizontally across the pins. Keep the knot against the left-hand pin.

3. Lay the second pair of Schnürli across the adjacent set of pins to lay parallel to the first.

4. Lay the third pair of Schnürli across the next adjacent set of pins.

5. Take a fourth single length of Schnürli and hold the short end on the left-hand side of the wheel above the top horizontal Schnürli.

6. Thread it diagonally over, under and over the three rows of Schnürli to rest against the right-hand pin. *(Fig. 224)*

7. You can use sticky tape to hold the Schnürli in place.

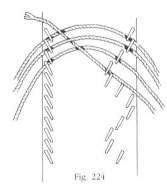

Fig. 224

Working

1. Mentally number the Schnürli from top to bottom, on the left L1 to L3, and on the right R1 to R4 from top to bottom.

2. Start working on the right-hand side of the wheel. Lift Schnürli R3.

3. Take Schnürli R1 over R2, under R3 and over R4. Lay the working end on the left below Schnürli L3. *(Fig. 225)*

4. Lower the raised end. There are three ends on the right and four on the left.

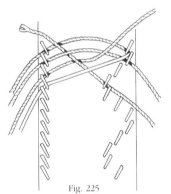

Fig. 225

5. Work the left-hand side. Raise Schnürli L3. Take L1 over L2, under L3, and over L4. Lay the working end on the right below R4. Lower the raised end.

6. Continue the working sequence gently tightening the Schnürli ends as you work. *(Fig. 226)*

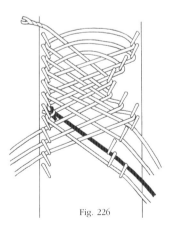

Fig. 226

7. When you have worked completely around the wheel carefully lift the beginning of the mesh off the pins and let it hang down behind the wheel.

Wheel Plait (Rädligeflecht)

Joining

1. Use a Weaver's knot, page 73, and space the joins evenly along the foot edge.

Finishing

1. Once the required length is made, loosely tie the ends. Once dry, the tie can be removed and the ends trimmed.

> **Handy hint**
> *Joining can be confusing when one end is attached to the wheel, so keep the attached old end on the left and cross it over the long end of new.*
> *Use the new end to make the knot.*

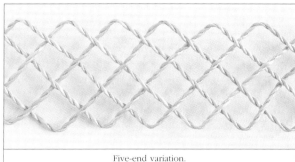

Five-end variation.

The Five-end variation being made on a narrow wheel.

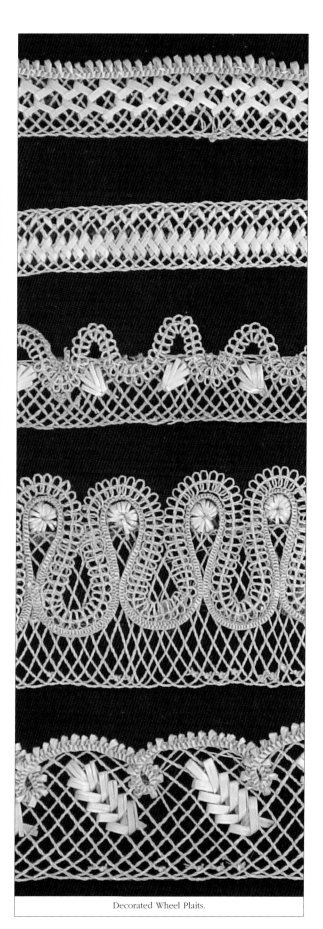

Decorated Wheel Plaits.

WHOLE STRAW

Preparation:	Selecting, Cutting, Storing, Dampening, Before you begin
Winding:	Broom, God's Eye, Wheat Ear, Leaf with Outline, Trefoil Leaf
Tying:	Star
Figure of Eight with one working end:	Horn
Cutting:	Pearls
Straw Plaits:	Making a Hat Plait
Swiss Speciality Plaits:	Shiny Tooth, Looped Shiny Tooth, Three-end Ring, Four-end Looped Ring, Four-end Fantasy Ring, Five-end Looped Ring, Five-end Double Looped Ring, Five-end Fantasy Ring, Eleven-end Ring
Other Hat Plaits:	Three-end Chain, Three-end Zig-Zag, Four-end Picot, Four-end Rustic, Six-end Rustic, Six-end Rustic Rose, Six-end Piping, Seven-end Plait

Preparation

Many of the motifs and some of the plaits included in this section were introduced into the Swiss straw industry comparatively late in its history. Whole straw was of limited use but when used it looked wonderful, providing a foil to the delicacy of both splints and Schnürli.

Selecting straw

Use either fine rye or wheat for the motifs and Swiss speciality plaits. Use wheat straw for the remaining plaits. Bleached straw is more flexible than natural straw so should be used when available. Some motifs are made using the complete top section of the straw (from below the head to first leaf joint).

Bleached straws.

Cutting

Look at the top section of the stem, it is thin at the head and thicker towards the leaf joint (node). Close to its mid-point the texture and colour of the straw changes. Remove the head, and then cut each straw at the point where the stem changes colour. The piece will be about 20–25cm (8–10") long.
Separate the straws into two groups, the tip (head/point/punte) ends, and the butt (foot/pedale) ends. Use only one type to make each motif or length of plait.
If you use the complete top section to make a plait then you must expect the width to vary. You can overcome this effect by starting the plait with a mixture of tip and butt ends, however you may find the straws more difficult to work.

Storing

Tie straws of similar thickness and type into small bundles and store in a box.

Dampening

Only soak enough straw for each working session.
Submerge the straws in hand-hot water for about ten minutes. When they are ready to use the thickest end of the straw will bend without cracking. Rye and some varieties of wheat may need a longer soaking time. Bleached and dyed straws may need a shorter soak.
Do not oversoak the straw, it will lose its colour and possibly be too soft to work successfully. Drain before use. Keep the straws damp during working.

Before you begin

When using split straw or Schnürli remember to work them whilst damp.
The diagrams do not necessarily show all completed moves.
Imperial measurements are usually approximate.

A hat decoration of Wheat Ear motifs.

Winding

Winding a whole straw around template pins can cause it to split so use very damp, fine straws and treat them with care as you bend them.

Broom (Beseli or Bäseli)

For your first attempts you may find it easier to make the first tie with thread and then over tie with the Schnürli. Always use evenly matched straws particularly when making a set of this motif.

You will need:
> 3 fine/medium straws, each 7cm (2.5")
> Thread, optional
> Schnürli 30cm (12")
> Darning needle

Starting

1. The straws must be tied so they lay side by side.
2. Use the Schnürli and tie the straws at the centre point with a half-knot. *(Fig. 227)*

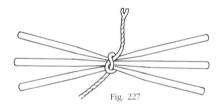

Fig. 227

Working

1. Fold the straws in half at the tie. Hold the short end of Schnürli toward the straw ends; it will be covered by the windings.
2. Starting at the folded end, wind the long end of the Schnürli around the straws. The first wind must be tight, pinching into the straw, to prevent slippage. *(Fig. 228)*
3. Make about 12 windings, gradually increasing each one to follow the angle of the straws.

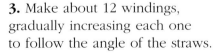

Fig. 228

Finishing

1. Put the needle diagonally through the work passing from inside the windings at the front to the back. *(Fig. 229)*
2. The point of the needle must emerge from the work two or three windings above the folded end. *(Fig. 230)*
3. Pull the Schnürli end through. Unthread the needle; adjust the windings. Use the long Schnürli end as a stem.
4. Trim the short end of Schnürli and shape the straw ends by cutting to a point or straight across.

Fig. 229

Fig. 230

Variation

Vary the shape by either cutting the straw ends to a point, or to dip towards the centre.

> ***Handy hint***
> *Do not start the winding too close to the folded end, it will slip off. If you are having problems, insert a small pin between the folded straws so that the winding cannot slip off.*

Winding

God's Eye (Motif mit Geteiltem Halm)

This motif enjoyed a relatively short period of popularity during the second half of the 1800s. Within the Swiss industry, God's Eyes were made from either splints or very fine whole straw.

You will need:
> 2 straws 5cm (2")
> 2 wires 5cm (2"), optional
> 1 straw 40cm (16")
> Thread, optional

Starting

1. To stiffen the motif, insert a wire into each of the short straws.
2. Cross the wired straws into a plus sign. Tie together using a transom knot. Once familiar with the technique omit the tying and hold the cross in place as you wind the straw.
3. Hold the end of the straw at the centre of the cross, leaving a 6mm (0.25") end.
4. Wind the long end anticlockwise around the top arm.

Working

1. Move the end in a clockwise direction to the next adjacent arm and wind around in an anticlockwise direction. *(Fig. 231)*

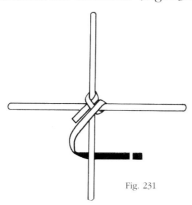

Fig. 231

2. Move clockwise to the next adjacent arm and wind the end around in an anticlockwise direction.
3. Ensure the crosspieces remain at 90° during working. Each row of winding slightly overlaps the previous one.
4. Continue the working sequence until the motif is 13–19mm (0.5"–0.75") square.

Finishing

1. The straw end must be at the front and laying on top of the next clockwise arm. Slide the end between last two rows of winding so the end is at the back. *(Fig. 232)*

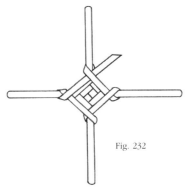

Fig. 232

2. Pull to tighten and at the same time correct the shape by gently pulling towards the outer edge of the motif. Once the motif is dry, trim the end.
3. Alternatively use thread to tie the straw end to an adjacent arm, then trim the end.
4. An alternative method of finishing is to use thread and tie the straw end to a crosspiece.
5. Cut each cross piece so that each is approximately 1mm longer than the winding.

The God's Eye on the left is made with whole straw whilst the other two are made from split straw.

Leaf shapes appear quite late in the industry, only being introduced early in the 20th century. They can be made in a variety of shapes. Always match the straw thickness to the size of leaf and only flatten the straw where it turns around a pin.

Wheat Ear (Halmenähre)

These instructions provide the method for making a leaf of any shape. If you want to shape the finished leaf insert a wire into the stem before stitching.

You will need:
>   2 straws each 40cm (16")
>   Template
>   Thread
>   Curved needle

Starting

1. Lay the first straw between the centre row of pins with the butt end forming a 3cm (1") long stem that protrudes from the bottom of the template.

Working

1. Using the long end, which is at the top of the template, work down the pins on the left-hand side. *(Fig. 233)*
2. Take the second straw, leave 3cm (1") of the tip end protruding from the bottom of the template. Work the straw up the right-hand set of pins. *(Fig. 234)*
3. Leave the end of the second straw pointing outwards from the top of the leaf. *(Fig. 235)*

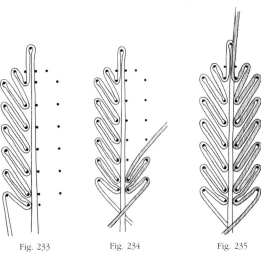

Fig. 233   Fig. 234   Fig. 235

Using a template where the pins are placed closer together, you can make a Wheat Ear with a Schnürli. The finished decoration (above) shows the Schnürli-Ähre motif with a Guffering outline.

Finishing

1. Using the thread make a tie between the first single and first pair of pins. Ensure that all the stems are included within the tie. Leave one long end of thread for finishing the rest of the motif. *(Fig. 236)*

Fig. 236

2. Now bend the central straw back over the tie to lay along the stem of the leaf. *(Fig. 237)*

3. Use a blanket (button-hole) stitch to fasten the leaf. *(Fig. 238)*

Fig. 237

4. Fasten the thread at the base of the leaf. Trim the second stem straw and the two ends from the points of the leaf just below the tie. *(Fig. 239)*

5. Carefully lift the leaf off the pins.

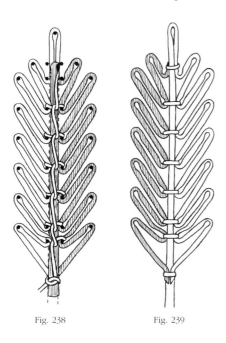

Fig. 238   Fig. 239

> ***Handy hint***
> *Use a soft thread for tying; it is less likely to cut through the straw.*

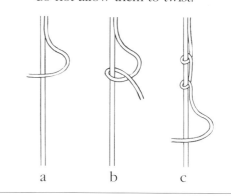

BLANKET STITCH

This stitch consists of a series of half hitches worked around a passive. As you make the stitches do not allow them to twist.

a   b   c

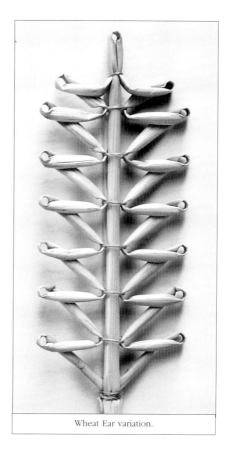

Wheat Ear variation.

Variation

Create a curl by turning the straw stem around the pin. You may need to use longer straws.

Winding

Leaf with Outline

This time the straws are worked in a different sequence. You will need to join a new straw into the old. For the best effect match the straws for colour and thickness.

You will need:

  2 or 3 straws, each 40cm (16")
  Template
  Thread
  Curved needle

Starting

1. Place the first straw so that the butt end protrudes 2 to 3cm (1") from the bottom of the template.

Working

1. Wind around the right-hand pins working from the bottom upwards.
2. Wind the straw around the top, central pin and bring the end down the centre, between the two rows of pins. *(Fig. 240)*
3. Work the same end around the left-hand set of pins, from bottom to top, and then bring the end back down between the two rows of pins. *(Fig. 241)*
4. Take the same end to the right-hand side of the shape and wind it around the outside of the leaf.

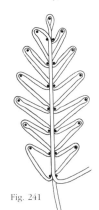

Fig. 240

Fig. 241

Joining

1. Cut the old straw to just below a pin and either insert the end of a new straw into the old straw or slide the new end over the old end.

Finishing

1. Secure with buttonhole stitches, working downwards from the top of the stem and then around the outside edge. *(Fig. 242)*
2. Lift the motif off the pins.
3. Trim the straw ends so that there is a single stem. Trim the thread ends.

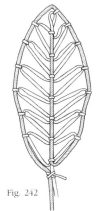

Fig. 242

These Little Stars of split straw and Schnürli are displayed on a whole straw outlined leaf.

Winding

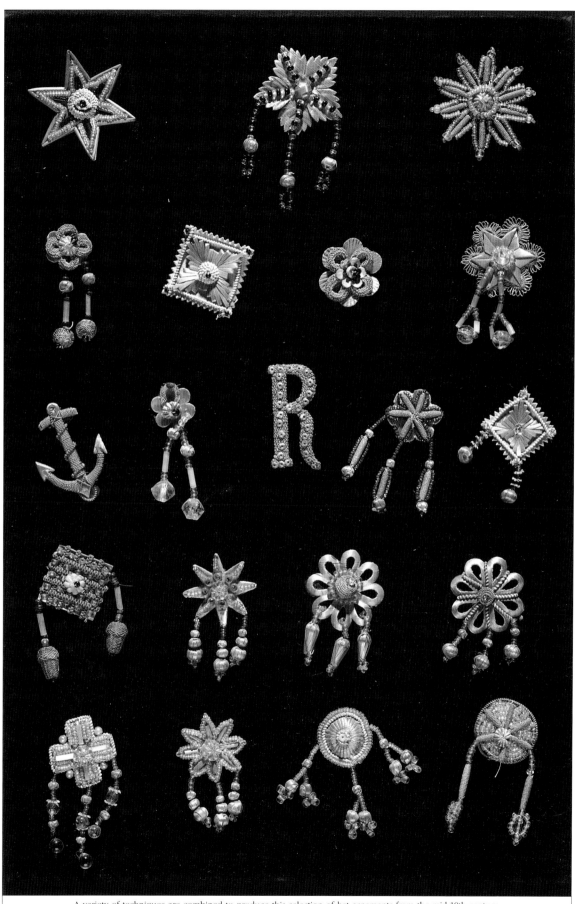

A variety of techniques are combined to produce this selection of hat ornaments from the mid-19th century.

Winding

Trefoil Leaf

If you intend to make or buy only one leaf board then this is the most versatile as the central section can be used independently. If you do not add an outline this leaf has a conifer-like appearance. You will need to join new straws to the old when making this leaf.

You will need:

> 5–6 straws, each 40cm (16")
> Template
> Thread
> Curved needle

Starting

1. The centre section is the first to be worked. Place the first straw so that the butt end protrudes 2 to 3cm (1") from the bottom of the template.

Working

1. Work around the right-hand pins of the centre section winding from bottom to top. *(Fig. 243)*

Fig. 243

2. Bring the end down between the two rows of pins to the bottom of the template.

3. Work around the pins on the left-hand side of the centre section. *(Fig. 244)*

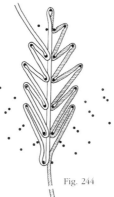

Fig. 244

4. Bring the end back to the bottom. *(Fig. 245)*

5. Take a new straw and work the left-hand section by following the Working steps 1 to 4. *(Fig. 246)*

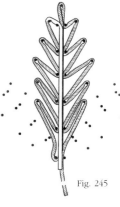

Fig. 245

6. Use a new straw to work the right-hand section following Working steps 1 to 4.

7. The same straw end is used to make the leaf outline so it may be necessary to join at this point.

Fig. 246

Joining

1. Follow the instructions for Leaf with Outline.

Finishing

1. Tie the thread around the top central leaf. Work from top to bottom using buttonhole stitches to fasten the leaf. *(Fig. 247)*

2. Fasten the end.

Fig. 247

3. Tie a second thread to the top of the right-hand leaf, work to the base then continue outwards along the left-hand leaf. Fasten the end.

4. Tie a thread to the central part of the base and begin to attach the outline straw, positioning the straw as you make the stitch. If you want a pointed tip on each leaflet keep the stitch to one side of the top pin. *(Fig. 248)*

Fig. 248

5. Work around the whole leaf. Fasten securely.

6. Lift the leaf off the pins.

7. Trim the straw and thread ends.

Tumbling leaves.

Star (Stern)

The eight-point star was used as a base for a flower-like motif, with an Air motif as the centre.

You will need:
> 4 fine/medium straws, 5cm (2")
> Thread

Starting

1. Use two straws to make a plus sign *(Fig 249)*. Hold in place by pressing on the crossing point.
2. Place the two straws on top, forming a multiplication sign. *(Fig. 250)*
3. Hold in place.

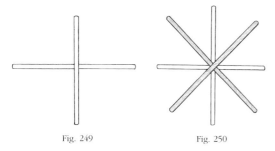

Fig. 249   Fig. 250

Working

1. Work the thread over and under the ends, passing the thread under the plus sign straws and over the multiplication sign straws. *(Fig. 251)*
2. Tie the thread ends with a half-knot, pulling tight so that the straws are held in place.

Finishing

1. Adjust the straws so equal lengths radiate from the tie.
2. Tighten the thread again and secure with a second knot.
3. If necessary trim the straw ends.

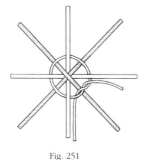

Fig. 251

FLOWER MOTIF

Swiss workers incorporated the motif as they tied the star, which is a confusing method so add the Air motif to the finished star. Use a 20mm (0.75") diameter, eight-point star and using a needle and thread stitch an Air motif, with stem, to the centre of the star.

Flower motifs.

Figure of Eight with one working end

As the straws are wound, stresses create a tendency to split. Minimise the risk by choosing fine flexible straw and avoid additional twisting as you work the figure of eight movement.

Horn (Hörnli)

This motif can also be worked with split straw or with Schnürli. Use this technique to make a leaf, bending the wire to shape as you work.

You will need:
Wire, 9cm (3.5")
One fine straw, 9cm (3.5")
One fine straw, 35cm (14")
Needle

Starting

1. Insert the wire into the short straw then bend the wire into a hairpin shape. *(Fig. 252)*
2. Fold the thin end of the long straw over the centre of the bend, leaving an end of about 13mm (0.5") laid against the wired straw. *(Fig. 253)*

Fig. 252

Fig. 253

Working

1. Start working the figure of eight pattern working towards the open end and enclosing the starting end. *(Fig. 254)*
2. Do not pull the straw too tightly against the wired straw.
3. Make approximately 10 complete moves; you can make more if the straw is longer.

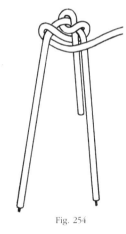

Fig. 254

Finishing

1. Insert the needle through the stitches alongside the wire at the open end. Bring the point out about 4 stitches from the end.
2. Thread the straw through the needle eye. *(Fig. 255)*
3. Carefully pull the end through the stitches.
4. Once dry, cut off the straw end and then cut away the surplus wired straw leaving about 1mm protruding.

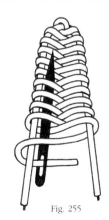

Fig. 255

Cutting

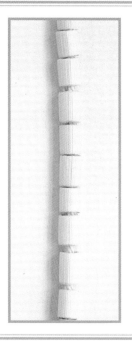

Pearls (Strohperlen or Strohschmelz)

Bleached or dyed rye straw is more robust than wheat straw and less likely to split when cut in this way. Long threaded lengths of Pearls can be added to a surface by using couching stitches to secure them. To use Pearls singly, first dampen slightly while still on the needle and attach each one using a very soft thread.

You will need:

Bleached or dyed straws 18–20cm (7–8")
Mattress needle 20–23cm (8–9")
Soft yarn
2B pencil, optional
Craft knife
Cutting board
Measuring rule

Starting

1. Cut a length of soft yarn approximately 10cm (4") longer than the straw.
2. Thread the yarn into the needle eye.
3. Push the needle into the straw, it must fit snugly around the needle. The point and eye must protrude from the straw.

Working

1. Lay the straw on a cutting surface.
2. You may wish to mark the straw at 5mm (0.25") intervals before starting to cut.
3. Use a sharp craft knife to carefully cut around the stem.
4. Cut beads from the whole length of straw.

Finishing

1. Gently pull the threaded needle through the straw.
2. Remove the needle from the yarn.
3. Knot the yarn at each end.

> ### Handy hint
> *If the Pearls break as you cut them the problem may be:*
> *The fit of the needle into the straw may be too loose.*
> *The type of straw may be too brittle.*
> *The sharpness of the knife may be too blunt.*

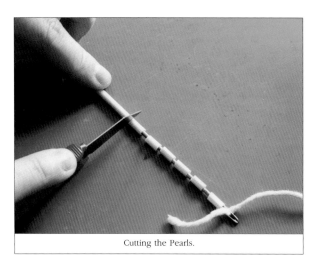

Cutting the Pearls.

A tassel of straw Pearls.

Straw Plaits (Stroh Geflechte)

In the 19th century, plaiters produced these plaits in fifty metre lengths! Their plaits were beautiful to look at and quick to make because they developed a specific working method which included joining new straws at regular intervals.

Making a Hat Plait

To be successful follow the traditional working techniques by holding the straws in both hands with the ends of the working straws pointing upwards and the plait hanging downwards.

You will need:

Straws as indicated in the individual instructions

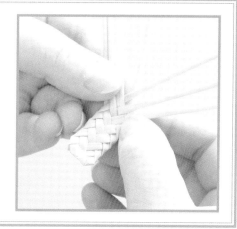

Starting

1. Fold the straws as directed, arranging them so that each end is a different length. It will help you to space joins evenly along the length. Or tie together the appropriate number of whole straws as indicated by the plait name.

2. Hold the straws in both hands.

Working

1. Manipulate the straws by using the thumb and first two fingers of each hand, using your left hand for the left side and right hand for the right.

2. Minimise your finger movements; twist the plait so that the working end slides between the straws in a scissor movement. When you begin the method may feel awkward, but persevere.

3. Edge patterns are normally, but not always, made along the left-hand edge (head).

Joining

1. Joins are only made along the right-hand edge (foot) or into the centre (body) of the plait. The instructions show only some of the possible joining options.

2. The straw being added must be the same width as the old end.

3. Avoid making joins in successive moves.

4. The old and new ends are clipped off once the plait is finished.

Finishing

1. Make a temporary tie or secure with a clip. Once the straws are dry the tie can be removed and the ends can be cut.

> **Handy hint**
> *Practice the plait moves by using paper strips.*

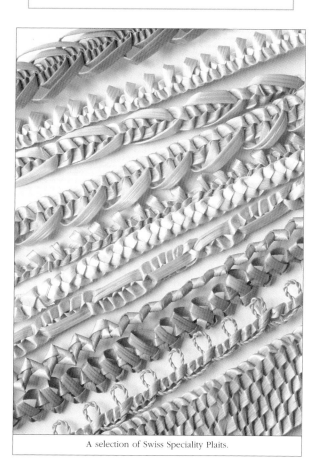

A selection of Swiss Speciality Plaits.

Swiss Speciality Plaits

Glanz-Zaggli and Ring plaits were specialities of the Swiss industry. They were normally made from rye 1mm straw splints but as you begin to make these plaits start by using whole straws or wide (3–5mm) straw splints. When using splints the shiny side must be kept to the outside and the diagrams show the folding movements necessary to achieve this effect. In the diagrams the splint's pith side is shaded.

Shiny Tooth (Glanz-Zaggli)

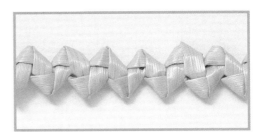

This plait has a saw-tooth appearance along both edges and is worked around a passive, which can be a cotton thread, a fine string, or wire. As you work hold the passive under tension.

You will need:
>1 straw
>Passive thread

Starting

1. Fold a straw off centre and put it around the passive with both ends pointing to the right. *(Fig. 256)*.
2. Hold it in place against the passive.
3. You can also start by tying two straws to the passive.

Fig. 256

Working

1. Take the end in front of the passive. Fold it under, away from you and then fold upwards so that it lays parallel to the right of the passive. *(Fig. 257)*

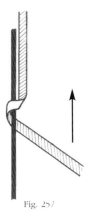

Fig. 257

2. Take the second end and fold it towards you and then upwards, in front of the first end to also lay parallel to the right of the passive. *(Fig. 258)*

Fig. 258

3. Fold the same end under and then sideways to the left passing in front of the other end and behind the passive to lay at a right angle. *(Fig. 259)*

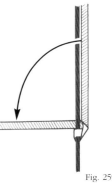

Fig. 259

Rosette made of Three-end Ring plait.

Swiss Speciality Plaits

4. Bring the second
end down in front of
the passive to lay to
the left. *(Fig. 260)*

Fig. 260

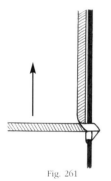

Fig. 261

5. Fold the same end
under and then upwards
to lay parallel to the left
of the passive. *(Fig. 261)*

6. Fold the second end
upwards in front of the
first. *(Fig. 262)*

Fig. 262

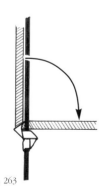

Fig. 263

7. Fold the same end
under and then side-
ways to lay to the right,
passing in front of the
other end and behind
the passive. *(Fig. 263)*

8. Fold the second end to across to the right.
9. Continue the Working sequence.

Joining

1. The horizontal straw is joined at Working
step 3. The vertical is joined at Working step
1 using the variations
shown in italics.
2. Insert the new straw
behind the old so it is
trapped behind the old
end and passive and in
front of the upright end.
(Fig. 264)
(Fig. 265).
3. Fold the short end of
the new straw down-
wards.
To the left.
4. Follow Working step 4.
Working step 2.
5. Follow Working step 5.
Working step 3.
6. Follow Working step 6,
Working step 4,
folding the old and new ends
together.
7. Follow Working step 7,
Working step 5,
folding only the new end.
8. Follow Working step 8,
Working step 6,
first folding the old end and cutting it off the
level with the right-hand edge of the passive,
top edge of the horizontal,
before folding the second end to the right.
9. Continue the Working sequence.

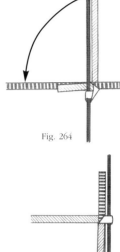

Fig. 264

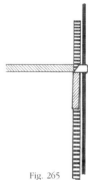

Fig. 265

Finishing

1. Tie the ends together or secure with a
clip until dry. Once dry the ends will stay
in place.
2. Clip off the joined ends once the plait
is dry.

Swiss Speciality Plaits

Looped Shiny Tooth (Gufezaggli)

This variation of the Shiny Tooth plait is made with a loop along one edge. The diagrams show how to make the loops using a form, which traditionally was a hairpin. After practice, the plaits can be made without using a form.

You will need:
> 1 straw
> Passive thread
> 2mm diameter form: cable needle or similar, optional

Starting

1. Fold the straw, off centre, around the passive.
2. Hold the form to the right of the straw and passive.

Working

1. Follow the working method for the Shiny Tooth plait. *(Fig. 266)*
2. Replace Working step 3 with the following move. Bring the back end around the form to the front then pass it to the left, between the upright end and passive. *(Fig. 267)*

Joining

1. Use the Shiny Tooth method.

Finishing

1. Fasten the ends until dry. Clip off the joined ends once the finished plait is dry.

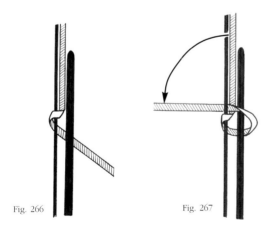

Fig. 266   Fig. 267

> **Handy hint**
> *As you work, pull the form towards the working end.*

This delicate hat ornament is decorated with Three-end Ring and Shiny Tooth plaits.

Swiss Speciality Plaits

A New Life by Brigitte Kilchmann, St. Silvester, Switzerland.

Swiss Speciality Plaits

Three-end Ring (Drei-Halm Ring)

The attractive appearance of this plait depends upon each fold being made at an angle of 120°. Visualise the angles by imagining a clock face; to help you the diagrams for the working sequence are shown against one. Use thick whole straws for your first attempts and progress to finer straws and splints. These instructions show one of the traditional starting methods, another is shown elsewhere.

You will need:

    2 straws

Starting

1. Fold one straw, off centre to form a 'v' shape with the ends at 11 and 1 o'clock.
2. Lay a second straw inside the 'v' parallel to the 1 o'clock end. *(Fig. 268)*
3. Fold the inside right-hand end downwards to 5 o'clock. *(Fig. 269)*
4. Fold the right-hand end of the 'v' downwards to 7 o'clock. *(Fig. 270)*
5. Fold the 5 o'clock end diagonally to lay to the right of the 11 o'clock end. *(Fig. 271)*
6. Rotate the work clockwise so that the two ends at 11 move to 12 o'clock.

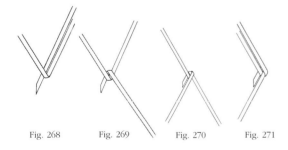

Fig. 268   Fig. 269   Fig. 270   Fig. 271

Working

1. Fold the left-hand 12 o'clock end across to 4 o'clock. *(Fig. 272)*
2. Fold the 8 o'clock end up to the left of the 12 o'clock end. *(Fig. 273)*
3. Fold the right-hand 12 o'clock end across to 8 o'clock. *(Fig. 274)*
4. Fold the 4 o'clock end up to the right of the 12 o'clock end. *(Fig. 275)*
5. Continue the Working sequence.

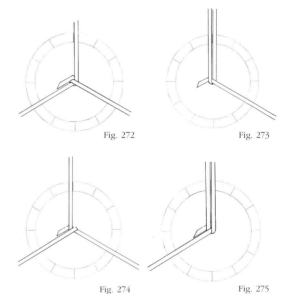

Fig. 272   Fig. 273

Fig. 274   Fig. 275

Joining

1. Join at Working step 1.
2. Lay the new straw over the old end. The short end of the new straw points towards 10 o'clock. *(Fig. 276)*
3. Continue the Working sequence until step 4 when the old end is left out of the plait.

Finishing

1. Fasten the ends until dry. Clip off the joined ends once the finished plait is dry.

Fig. 276

Swiss Speciality Plaits

Four-end Looped Ring (Vier-Halm Gufering)

Although the plait looks complicated it is in fact a very simple variation of the basic Ring plait. The addition of a fourth straw allows you to create a small loop along one edge. The loops form naturally without the use of a form, but for your first attempts you may wish to use one.

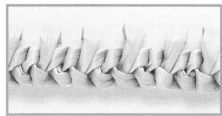

You will need:

> 3 straws
> 2mm diameter form: cable needle or similar, optional

Starting

1. Take three straws. Hold one vertically and part way along the length, (towards, but not in the centre) lay the other two straws on top so that the long ends are at 4 o'clock. *(Fig. 277)*

2. Fold the lower part of the vertical straw up to lay to the left of the original 12 o'clock end. Fold the two short ends, from 4 o'clock, downwards. *(Fig. 278)*

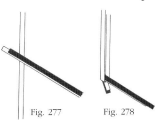

Fig. 277   Fig. 278

Working

1. Fold the right-hand 12 o'clock end to 8 o'clock. *(Fig. 279)*

2. Fold both straws at 4 o'clock up to right-hand 12 o'clock. *(Fig. 280)*

3. Fold the left-hand 12 o'clock end to 4 o'clock. *(Fig. 281)*

4. Fold the 8 o'clock end up to left-hand 12 o'clock. *(Fig. 282)*

5. Fold both right-hand 12 o'clock straws to 8 o'clock. *(Fig. 283)*

6. Fold the 4 o'clock end up to right-hand 12 o'clock. *(Fig. 284)*

7. Fold the left-hand 12 o'clock end to 4 o'clock. *(Fig. 285)*

8. Fold only the uppermost straw at 8 o'clock to left-hand 12 o'clock. Now the ends are in position to form the loop. *(Fig. 286)*

9. Curl the second 8 o'clock end and bring it between the two 12 o'clock ends to lay on top of the existing 4 o'clock. *(Fig. 287)*

10. Continue the Working sequence.

Joining

1. Follow the instructions for Ring plait, joining at either Working step 3 or 7.

Finishing

1. Fasten the ends until dry. Clip off the joined ends once the finished plait is dry.

> ***Handy hint***
> *When using splints remember to turn the shiny side to the front. The face of the plait and outside of the loops will be shiny; the back of the plait will be matt.*

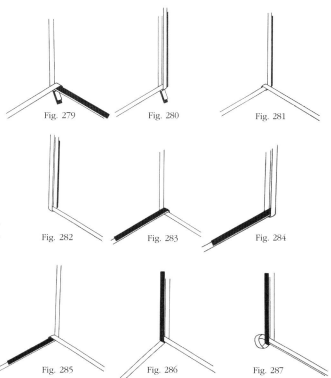

Fig. 279   Fig. 280   Fig. 281

Fig. 282   Fig. 283   Fig. 284

Fig. 285   Fig. 286   Fig. 287

Swiss Speciality Plaits

Four-end Fantasy Ring (Vier-Halm Phantasie-Ring)

In this plait the fourth end is used to form an elongated loop that covers part of the plait, first on the right and then on the left.

You will need:

    3 straws

Starting

1. Use the instructions for the Four-end Looped Ring.
2. Fold the right-hand 12 o'clock end to 8 o'clock. *(Fig. 288)*

Working

1. Fold only the uppermost 4 o'clock straw to the right-hand 12 o'clock. The second straw at 4 o'clock is left behind to form the first right-hand loop. *(Fig. 289)*
2. Work the following moves. Left-hand 12 to 4, 8 to left-hand 12, right-hand 12 to 8, top 4 to right-hand 12.
3. Repeat step 2. *(Fig. 290)*
4. Make the loop with the 4 o'clock straw that was left behind. Loosely curl the straw over the plait to rest on top of the right-hand 12 o'clock.
5. Fold the left-hand 12 o'clock end to 4 o'clock.
6. Fold the 8 o'clock end to left-hand 12 o'clock. *(Fig. 291)*
7. Fold both right-hand 12 o'clock ends to 8 o'clock.
8. Fold the 4 o'clock end to right-hand 12 o'clock. *(Fig. 292)*
9. Fold the left-hand 12 o'clock end to 4 o'clock.
10. Fold the uppermost straw at 8 o'clock to right-hand 12 o'clock.
The lower straw stays behind ready to make the next loop. *(Fig. 293)*
11. Work the following moves. Right-hand 12 to 8, 4 to right-hand 12, left-hand 12 to 4, top 8 to left-hand 12.
12. Repeat step 11.
13. Make the loop with the 8 o'clock straw that was left behind. Loosely curl it over the plait to lay on top of the left-hand 12 o'clock end.
14. Fold the right-hand 12 o'clock end to 8 o'clock. *(Fig. 294)*

15. Fold the 4 o'clock end to right-hand 12 o'clock.
16. Fold both ends at left-hand 12 o'clock to 4 o'clock.
17. Fold the 8 o'clock end to left-hand 12 o'clock. *(Fig. 295)*
18. Fold the right-hand 12 o'clock end to 8 o'clock.
19. Continue the Working sequence.

Joining

1. Follow the Ring plait instructions to join into the body of the plait during either Working step 2 or 3.
2. Join a new straw on to the loop at Working step 4 inserting the new straw behind the old. Work both old and new ends until Working step 7. At Working step 13 leave the old end behind.

Finishing

1. Fasten the ends until dry. Clip off the joined ends once the finished plait is dry.

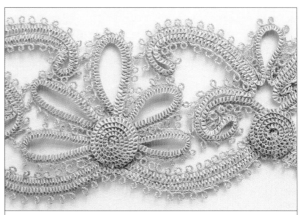

Made in long lengths, this decoration would have been stitched to a fabric bonnet.

Swiss Speciality Plaits

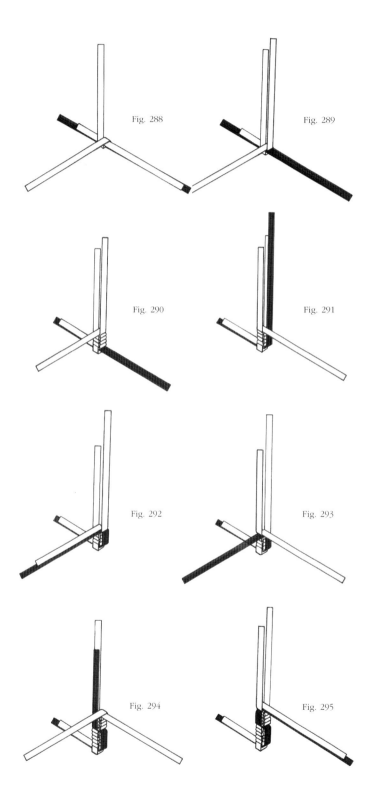

Fig. 288

Fig. 289

Fig. 290

Fig. 291

Fig. 292

Fig. 293

Fig. 294

Fig. 295

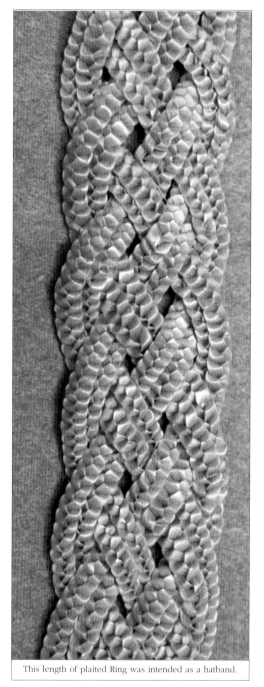

This length of plaited Ring was intended as a hatband.

Swiss Speciality Plaits

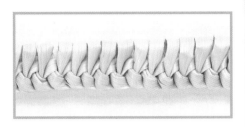

Five-end Looped Ring (Fünf-Halm Gufenring)

The extra working end allows you to make a loop on each left-hand move creating a luscious looking plait.

You will need:
4 straws
2mm diameter form: cable needle or similar, optional

Starting

1. Hold two straws, one on top of the other so that they point from 10 o'clock to 4 o'clock.
2. Place one straw behind, off centre and about 2cm (0.75") from the 10 o'clock end so that it points from 8 o'clock to 2 o'clock.
3. Place a 2nd straw behind with only 2cm (0.75") pointing towards 8 o'clock. *(Fig. 296)*
4. Fold the long 8 o'clock end to 12 o'clock.
5. Fold both straws at 2 o'clock to 8 o'clock.
6. Fold both 4 o'clock straws to right-hand 12 o'clock. *(Fig. 297)*

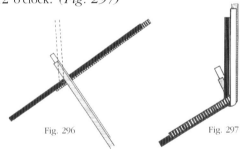

Fig. 296   Fig. 297

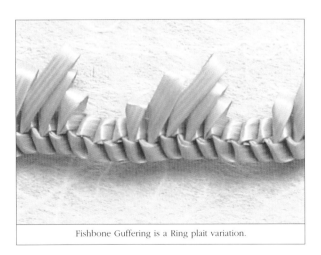

Fishbone Guffering is a Ring plait variation.

Working

1. Fold the single left-hand 12 o'clock end to 4 o'clock.

2. Fold only the uppermost straw at 8 o'clock to 12 o'clock. *(Fig. 298)*

Fig. 298

3. Make the first loop by curling the lower 8 o'clock straw around the left-hand 12 o'clock end to lay at 4 o'clock. *(Fig. 299)*

Fig. 299

4. Fold both right-hand 12 o'clock ends to 8 o'clock.

5. Fold both 4 o'clock ends up to the right-hand 12 o'clock. *(Fig. 300)*

6. Continue the Working sequence.

Fig. 300

Joining

1. Follow the Ring plait instructions, joining at Working step 1.

Finishing

1. Fasten the ends until dry. Clip off the joined ends once the finished plait is dry.

Swiss Speciality Plaits

Five-end Double Looped Ring (Fünf-Halm Gufen Phantasie)

This time the working sequence creates two loops, one inside the other along the left-hand edge.

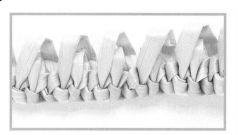

You will need:

> 4 straws
> 2mm diameter form: cable needle or similar, optional

Starting

1. Use the instructions for the Five-end Looped Ring.
2. Fold the single left-hand 12 o'clock end to 4 o'clock.
3. Fold only the uppermost 8 o'clock end to left-hand 12 o'clock.
4. Fold the two right-hand 12 o'clock ends to 8 o'clock. *(Fig. 301)*

Fig. 301

Working

1. Fold the single 4 o'clock end to right-hand 12 o'clock. *(Fig. 302)*
2. Fold the single left-hand 12 o'clock end to 4 o'clock. *(Fig. 303)*
3. There are three straws stacked in the 8 o'clock position. Fold the uppermost end to 12 o'clock.
4. Make the first loop. Take the next (uppermost) 8 o'clock straw, curl it behind the left-hand 12 o'clock end to 4 o'clock. One end remains at 8 o'clock. *(Fig. 304)*
5. Fold the right-hand 12

Fig. 302

Fig. 303

Fig. 304

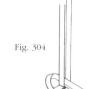

---

o'clock end to 8 o'clock. *(Fig. 305)*
6. Fold both straws at 4 o'clock to right-hand 12 o'clock.
7. Fold the left-hand 12 o'clock straw to 4 o'clock.
8. Fold the uppermost 8 o'clock straw to 12 o'clock. *(Fig. 306)*
9. Make the second loop. Take the 8 o'clock straw and curl behind the left-hand 12 o'clock end to 4 o'clock. *(Fig. 307)*
10. Fold both right-hand 12 o'clock ends to 8 o'clock.
11. Fold both 4 o'clock ends to right-hand 12 o'clock.
12. Fold the left-hand 12 o'clock end to 4 o'clock.
13. Fold only the uppermost 8 o'clock straw to 12 o'clock.
14. Fold both right-hand 12 o'clock ends to 8 o'clock.
15. Continue the Working sequence.

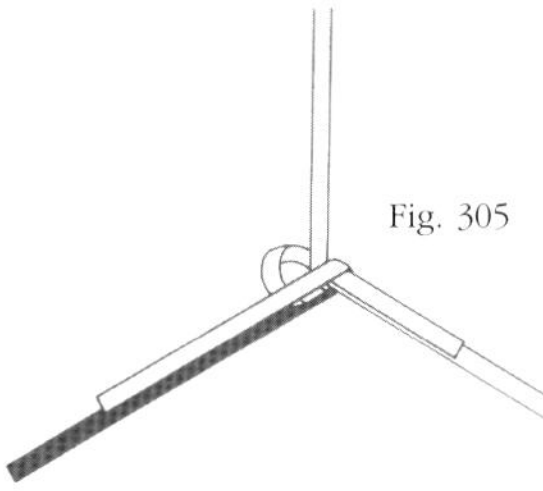

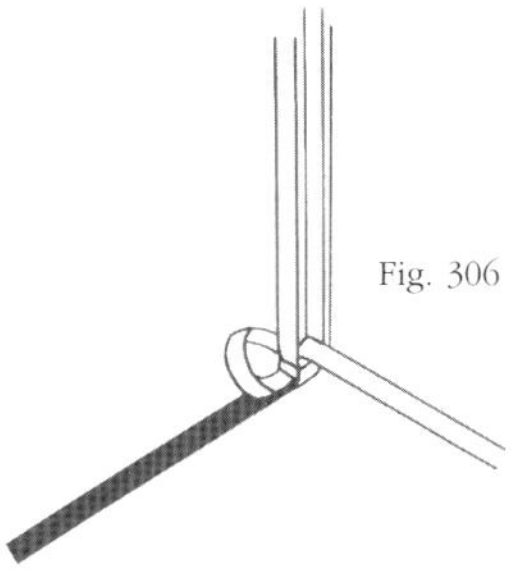

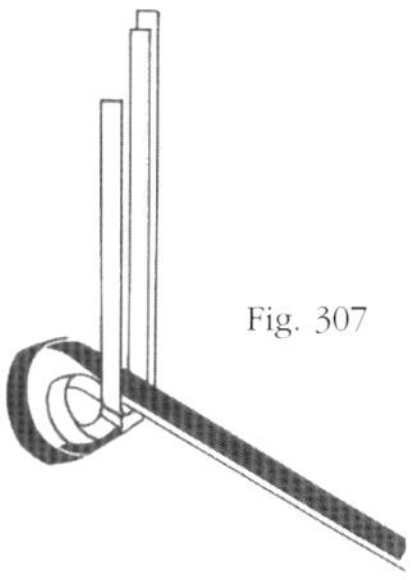

Fig. 305

Fig. 306

Fig. 307

Joining

1. Follow the Ring Plait instructions, joining at Working steps 2 or 7 or 12.

Finishing

1. Fasten the ends until dry. Clip off the joined ends once the finished plait is dry.

Swiss Speciality Plaits

Five-end Fantasy Ring (Fünf-Halm Ring Phantasie)

In this version the loops are formed along both edges.

You will need:
  4 straws
  2mm diameter form: cable needle or
  similar, optional

Starting

1. Arrange the straws as shown. *(Fig. 308)*
2. Fold the long end at 8 o'clock up to the
12 o'clock position. *(Fig. 309)*
3. Fold the two ends at 2 o'clock to 8 o'clock.
(Fig. 310)

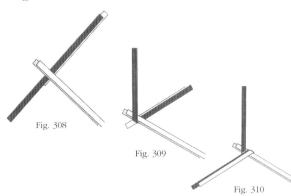

Fig. 308

Fig. 309

Fig. 310

Working

1. Fold the uppermost straw at 4 o'clock to
right-hand 12 o'clock.
2. Fold the left-hand 12 o'clock end to the
4 o'clock position.
3. Fold the uppermost straw at 8 o'clock to
left-hand 12 o'clock.
4. Work the following moves. Single right-
hand 12 to 8, top 4 to 12, left-hand 12 to 4,
top 8 to left-hand 12.
5. Repeat step 4.
6. Make the left-hand
loop. Fold the lowest
8 o'clock end up and curl
behind the left-hand 12
o'clock to lay at 4 o'clock.
(Fig. 311)

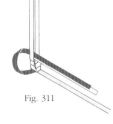

Fig. 311

7. Fold the right-hand
12 o'clock end to 8
o'clock.
8. Fold the uppermost
straw at 4 o'clock to 12
o'clock. *(Fig. 312)*
9. Make the right-hand
loop. Fold the lowest
4 o'clock end upward
and curl behind the
right-hand 12 o'clock
end to lay at 8 o'clock.
(Fig. 313)
10. Fold the left-hand
12 o'clock end to 4
o'clock. *(Fig. 314)*
11. The lowest end of
the two at 8 o'clock and
the lowest end of the
two at 4 o'clock are left
behind ready to form the next loops.
12. Fold the uppermost 8 o'clock straw to left-
hand 12 o'clock.
13. Fold the right-hand 12 o'clock end to
8 o'clock.
14. Continue the Working sequence.

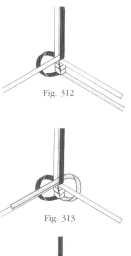

Fig. 312

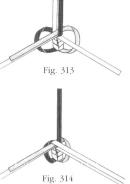

Fig. 313

Fig. 314

Joining

1. Follow the Ring Plait instructions, joining
at Working step 4.

Finishing

1. Fasten the ends until dry. Clip off the
joined ends once the finished plait is dry.

Swiss Speciality Plaits

Eleven-end Ring

This is just one of a large family of similar wide plaits originally made from split straw. Whole straws are easier to work but unfortunately the plait will lose some of its delicacy. To simplify the working sequence instructions the diagrams show numbered ends.

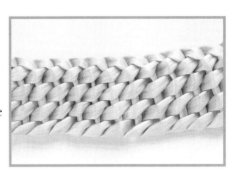

You will need:

  6 straws

Starting

1. Hold one straw horizontally with the long end pointing to the left.
2. Starting about 3cm (1.25") from the right-hand end of the horizontal wrap a straw around.
3. Repeat with the remaining straws making sure the ends are different lengths. *(Fig. 315)*
4. Fold the horizontal straw across the group of five. *(Fig. 316)*

6. Fold the horizontal end upwards to lay to the right of the last right-hand diagonal. Note the angle of the fold. *(Fig. 317)*
7. Fold the top left-hand diagonal end (marked *) to the horizontal position. Note the angle of the fold. *(Fig. 318)*
8. Repeat the Working sequence.

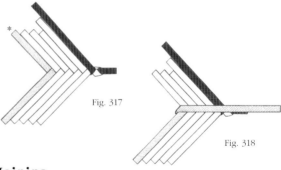

Fig. 317

Fig. 318

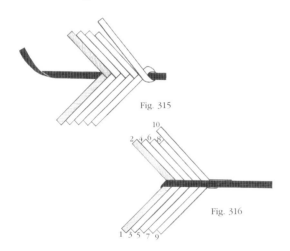

Fig. 315

Fig. 316

Working

1. Fold end #1 upwards to lay to the left of #2.
2. Fold #2 down to lay in the space vacated by #1.
3. Fold end #3 upwards to lay to the left of #4.
4. Fold #4 down to lay in the space vacated by #3.
5. Repeat with the remaining ends.

Joining

1. Add a new straw over the old horizontal end. *(Fig. 319)*
2. Straws can be added diagonally but the result may not be as attractive as the old and new ends must be worked together for several moves.

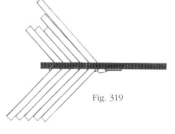

Fig. 319

Finishing

1. Fasten the ends until dry. Clip off the joined ends once the finished plait is dry.

Other Hat Plaits

Some of these plaits, such as the Four-end Rustic, can be dated back to the European hat industries of the 17th century whilst others were not introduced until late in the 19th century. We'll never know in which country each plait originated, such was the intensity of copying between the various plaiting centres. These plaits were made from either whole or split straw, sometimes the straws were bleached, more commonly the plaits were made by mixing a variety of brightly dyed straws.

Three-end Chain

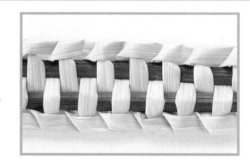

If you want to copy the original sample in the Freiämter Stroh Museum, use chenille as the passives or use whole dyed straw.

You will need:

2 straws, same width as the passives
2 passives *
* Use two separate passives or fold one long length in half making a 'u' shape

Starting

1. Insert one straw off centre into the 'u', passing it in front of the left-hand and behind the right-hand passive. Both ends of this straw must be long.

2. Insert the second straw above the first, passing behind the left-hand and in front of the right-hand passive. Keep the short end on the right. *(Fig. 320)*

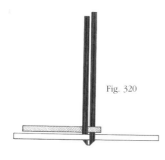
Fig. 320

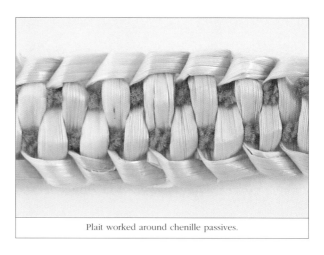
Plait worked around chenille passives.

3. Fold the lowest left-hand end under, away from you, making a diagonal crease in the straw. Then fold it upwards, passing under the remaining left-hand horizontal end to lay parallel to the left-hand passive.

4. Fold the same straw forward, making a diagonal crease, to lay at a right angle to the two passives, then pass it over the left and under the right-hand passive. *(Fig. 321)*

Fig. 321

5. Fold the remaining left-hand horizontal end towards you and upwards, making a diagonal crease, then lay it parallel to the left-hand passive. *(Fig. 322)*

6. Fold the lower horizontal right-hand end upwards, making a diagonal crease, then pass it behind the other right-hand horizontal to lay parallel to the right-hand passive.

Fig. 322

Other Hat Plaits

Working

1. Fold the right-hand vertical towards you, making a diagonal crease, so it lays at a right angle to the passives then pass it over, under, over the verticals (two passives and left-hand vertical end). *(Fig. 323)*

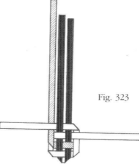

Fig. 323

2. Fold the remaining right-hand horizontal end upwards towards you, making a diagonal crease, to lay parallel to the right-hand passive.

3. Work the left-hand vertical straw. Fold it towards you, making a diagonal crease, then pass it through verticals in an over, under, over sequence. *(Fig. 324)*

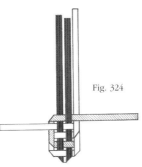

Fig. 324

4. Fold the left-hand horizontal straw towards you and upwards, making a diagonal crease, to lay parallel to the left-hand passive.

5. Continue the Working sequence.

Joining

1. Join at Working step 1. Leave the old end behind when the new straw is folded to the vertical position. *(Fig. 325)*

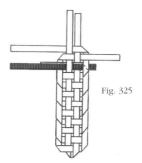

Fig. 325

2. Join on to a passive by either inserting a new end into the old end of the straw, or overlaying old and new.

Finishing

1. Fasten the ends until dry. Clip off the joined ends once the finished plait is dry.

A selection of hat plaits.

Other Hat Plaits

Three-end Zig-Zag

This plait can be made with a rounded outline as shown in the diagrams or as a defined zig-zag by carefully folding the working straw to a point as described in the Shiny Tooth instructions.

You will need:

    2 straws, same width as the passives
    2 passives, prepared as for Three-end Chain

Starting

1. Insert the working ends as shown so that there are three ends pointing to the left. (*Fig. 326*)

Working

1. Fold the lowest left-hand end under then upwards, making a diagonal crease. Pass it under and over the two remaining left-hand horizontal ends. (*Fig. 327*)

2. Fold the lower left-hand end under then upwards, making a diagonal crease. Pass it behind the remaining horizontal straw to lay parallel to the left-hand vertical. (*Fig. 328*)

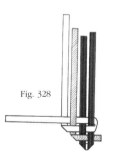

3. Twist (or fold to form a point) the remaining left-hand horizontal end to pass under, over, under and over the verticals. (*Fig. 329*)

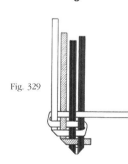

4. Fold the outside left-hand vertical under to make a diagonal crease, then pass it under, over, under the remaining vertical to lay parallel to the top right-hand horizontal.

5. Fold the remaining left-hand vertical under to make a diagonal crease then pass it under and over the two passives. (*Fig. 330*)

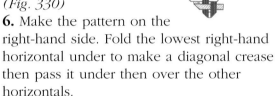

6. Make the pattern on the right-hand side. Fold the lowest right-hand horizontal under to make a diagonal crease then pass it under then over the other horizontals.

7. Fold the next horizontal in the same way passing under the remaining horizontal.

8. Twist (or fold to form a point) the remaining right-hand horizontal end under, make a diagonal crease and pass it through the verticals, under, over, under, over. (*Fig. 331*)

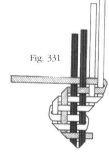

9. Fold the outside right-hand vertical under, make a diagonal crease then pass it under, over and under the remaining verticals.

10. Fold the remaining right-hand horizontal straw under to make a diagonal crease then pass it under and over the passives.

11. Continue the Working sequence.

Joining

1. Join on to a horizontal at either Working step 10 or 11.

Finishing

1. Fasten the ends until dry. Clip off the joined ends once the finished plait is dry.

Other Hat Plaits

Four-end Picot

This simple plait can be made using whole straw or single splints. If you want a lightweight strong plait use pairs of splints faced with the shiny side outwards. Keep the picots an even size by using a form. The width of the plait body should be the same as the width of the picot.

You will need:
    2 straws
    Flat form 5mm (0.25") wide, optional

Starting

1. Hold one straw horizontally and the second off centre diagonally (60°) behind with the top of the diagonal to the right. Fold the lower end of the straw upwards in front of the horizontal. *(Fig. 332)*
2. Fold the right-hand end of the horizontal straw diagonally over the right-hand straw. This end must lay on the inside of the 'v' shape.
3. Fold the left-hand arm of the 'v' diagonally to lay to the inside of the right-hand straw. *(Fig. 333)*
4. The left-hand end of the horizontal straw remains in its original position, ready to make the loop.
5. Fold the outside right-hand end over the remaining right-hand end. *(Fig. 334)*

Fig. 332   Fig. 333   Fig. 334

Working

1. Form the first picot. Fold the left-hand horizontal straw diagonally under, make a crease to form the point of the picot, then bring it into the plait passing under and then over the two left-hand straws. *(Fig. 335)*
2. Fold the outside right-hand end over the adjacent end. Lay it inside the left-hand

Fig. 335

group. There are three ends on the left. Fold the middle left-hand end over the inside left-hand end. *(Fig. 336)*
3. Fold the outside right-hand end over the next to lay to the inside of the left-hand group.
4. Continue the Working sequence and make the next picot. All picots should be the same size. *(Fig. 337)*

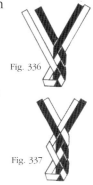

Fig. 336

Fig. 337

Joining

1. The straw to be joined must be in the outside right-hand position. Lay a new straw over the old, long end pointing to the right. Continue plaiting the new end, leave the old end behind. *(Fig. 338)*
2. Clip off the ends once the plait is dry.

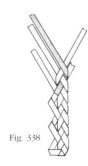

Fig. 338

Finishing

1. Fasten the ends until dry. Clip off the joined ends once the finished plait is dry.

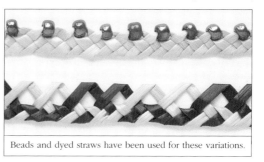

Beads and dyed straws have been used for these variations.

Other Hat Plaits

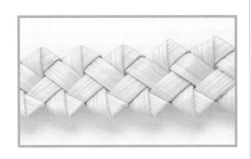

Four-end Rustic

As you work the rustic plaits the right side of the pattern faces away from you.

You will need:

    2 straws

Starting

1. Hold one straw horizontally and the second off centre diagonally (60°) behind with the top of the diagonal to the right. Fold the lower end of the straw upwards in front of the horizontal.

2. Fold the right-hand end of the horizontal straw diagonally over the right-hand arm of the 'v' to lay inside the left-hand arm. *(Fig. 339)*

3. Fold the left-hand end of the horizontal under the outside straw and over the next. *(Fig. 340)*

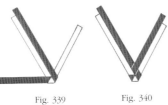

Fig. 339   Fig. 340

Working

1. Fold the outside right-hand end in front of the other straws, making a diagonal crease then pass it over the two centre straws and under the outside left-hand straw. *(Fig. 341)*

2. Fold the same end towards you and make a diagonal crease so that the end lays to the

inside of the right-hand arm of the 'v', make a crease. Now pass the same end over then under the two left-hand straws. *(Fig. 342)*

3. Fold the outside left-hand end across the front of the plait, making a diagonal crease, and then pass it over the two centre straws and under the outside right-hand straw. *(Fig. 343)*

4. Fold the same end towards you and diagonally upwards so that it lays to the inside of the left-hand arm of the 'v', make a crease. Pass the same end over and under the two right-hand straws. *(Fig. 344)*

5. Continue the Working sequence.

Handy hint
To produce a plait without gaps keep the angle of the 'v' shape at 60°.
At working steps 1 and 3 pull the end horizontal straw downwards to close the gap.

Joining

1. A new straw can be added on either Working step 1 (horizontal) or Working step 4 (diagonal). *(Figures 345 & 346)*

2. When the new straw is worked leave behind the old end.

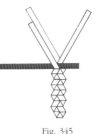 

Fig. 345   Fig. 346

Finishing

1. Fasten the ends until dry. Clip off the joined ends once the finished plait is dry.

Handy hint
The appearance of finished plaits, the ones that do not have a raised decorative edge, can be improved by milling.

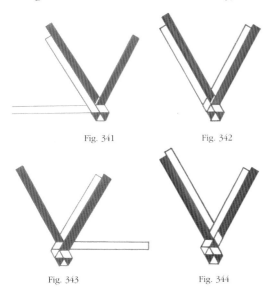

Fig. 341   Fig. 342

Fig. 343   Fig. 344

Other Hat Plaits

Six-end Rustic

The rustic plait can be made wider by the introduction of extra straws. Some of the Chinese and Japanese plaits exported to Europe early in the 20th century were made with sixteen ends.

You will need:

    3 straws

Starting

1. Fold three straws as shown in the diagram. *(Fig. 347)*

2. Fold the right-hand horizontal end upwards to lay to the inside of the left-hand 'v', make a crease. Pass the same end over the outside and then under the right-hand straw.

3. Fold the outside left-hand horizontal end diagonally upwards to lay to the inside of the right-hand arm of the 'v', make a crease. Move the same end over, under and then over the three left-hand straws. *(Fig. 348)*

Fig. 347

Fig. 348

Working

1. Start on the right-hand side. Follow the Four-end Rustic instructions, but this time the working end passes over four straws on the horizontal move. *(Fig. 349)*

2. Work the left-hand side. *(Fig. 350)*

3. Continue the Working sequence.

Fig. 349

Fig. 350

Joining

1. Follow the instructions for the Four-end Rustic.

Finishing

1. Fasten the ends until dry. Clip off the joined ends once the finished plait is dry.

Variation

To create a checkerboard effect on the body of the plait make the following adjustment. On the diagonal working move take the working end over one, under one, over one.

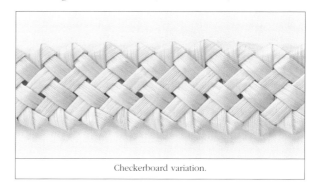

Checkerboard variation.

Other Hat Plaits

Six-end Rustic Rose

This very pretty plait is simple once you are familiar with the basic Six-end Rustic. The rose is made by folding the two outside right-hand straws in a circular sequence of moves.

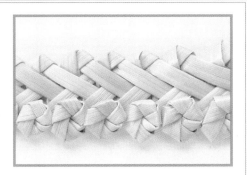

You will need:

    3 straws

Starting

1. Follow the instructions for starting the Six-end Rustic.
2. Fold the outside right-hand straw to its horizontal position. (*Fig. 351*)

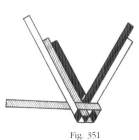
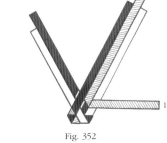

Fig. 351   Fig. 352   Fig. 353

Working

1. Turn the plait over to the right side, so that the working end is on the right. (*Fig. 352*)
2. Fold the right-hand horizontal straw, #1, diagonally under the outside right-hand straw, #2 and then over the remaining two straws on the right, pointing to the left and laying parallel to the two left-hand diagonal ends. (*Fig. 353*)
3. Fold the outside right-hand straw, #2, under the straw of the last move, #1, to lay horizontally across the face of the plait. (*Fig. 354*)
4. Fold straw, #1 under #2. (*Fig. 355*)
5. Fold straw #2 under #1. (*Fig. 356*)
6. Fold straw #1 under #2. (*Fig. 357*)
7. Fold straw #2 under #1. (*Fig. 358*)
8. Turn the plait over. The rose is on the left-hand underside. The next two moves fasten the rose into the plait.
9. Fold the horizontal straw, #1, diagonally upwards and then pass it over one, under two. (*Fig. 359*)
10. Fold the outside left-hand straw, #2, across the plait, making a diagonal crease, then pass it over the next four straws and under the outside right-hand straw.

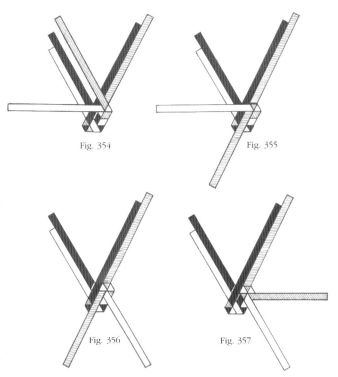

Fig. 354   Fig. 355

Fig. 356   Fig. 357

Other Hat Plaits

Continue the move by folding the same straw diagonally upwards over and then under the next two straws. *(Fig. 360)*

11. Fold the outside right-hand straw across the plait, over the next four straws and then under the outside left-hand straw. *(Fig. 361)*

12. Continue the Working sequence.

Joining

1. Follow the instructions for the Four-end Rustic.

Finishing

1. Fasten the ends until dry. Clip off the joined ends once the finished plait is dry.

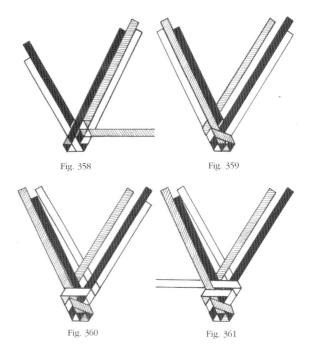

Fig. 358   Fig. 359

Fig. 360   Fig. 361

This graceful decoration must have looked wonderful on a summer bonnet.

Other Hat Plaits

Six-end Piping

The head edge of the plait is folded over a flat form. In the past, plaiters often used a whalebone taken from their corset! Reinforced packing tape makes a suitable substitute.

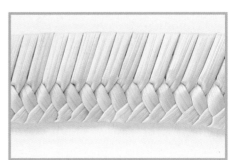

You will need:
>   3 straws
>   Flat form 3–5mm (0.25"), wide 10cm (4") long

Starting

1. Hold the form vertically and fold three straws around as shown. *(Fig. 362)*

Working

1. Fold the lowest straw over the next then under two and over the remaining straws. It must lay diagonally to the left of the form. Fold the same end under and around the form to lay, in line with the other straws, diagonally to the right of the form so that it becomes the top straw in the working group. *(Fig. 363)*
2. Repeat this move by using the lowest straw of the working group. *(Fig. 364)*
3. Keep the straws neatly folded around the form and make sure that they lay side by side. *(Fig. 365)*
4. Continue the working sequence.

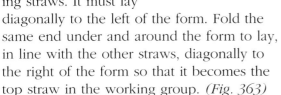

Fig. 362

Joining

1. Always add a new working straw on to the foot edge (right-hand).
2. The end to be joined must be second from the bottom of the working group. Lay the new end over the old.
3. Make the move with the lowest straw. The new end is secured by this move. *(Fig. 366)*
4. To join on to the form lay a new straw over the old end and hold in place until made secure by the work. Allow about 2cm (0.75") of overlap.

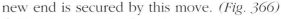

Fig. 366

Finishing

1. Fasten the ends until dry. Clip off the joined ends once the finished plait is dry.

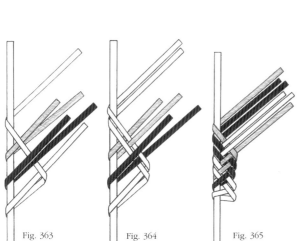

Fig. 363   Fig. 364   Fig. 365

Curve the plait to create a lacy edge effect.

Other Hat Plaits

Seven-end Plait

Even today this is one of the hat industry's most important plaits and is still made in many countries. Remember the working sequence by using this rhyme, *over one, under two, pull it tight and that will do.*

You will need:
  4 straws

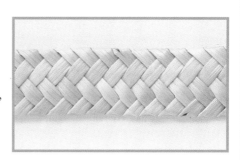

Starting

1. Take three straws and fold them as for the Six-end Rustic plait. Make sure that the ends are different lengths.

2. Take the fourth straw and lay it diagonally inside the right-hand arm of the 'v'. Leave a 2cm (1") end below the horizontal straw. *(Fig. 367)*

Fig. 367

3. Fold the right-hand end of the horizontal straw diagonally upwards to lay to the inside the left-hand arm of the 'v', make a crease. Pass the same end over the outside right-hand diagonal end and under the remaining two on the right. *(Fig. 368)*

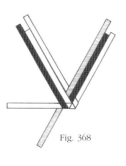

Fig. 368

4. Fold the left-hand end of the horizontal straw diagonally upwards to lay to the inside the right-hand arm of the 'v', make a crease. Pass the same end over the outside diagonal end and under the remaining two on the right-hand. *(Fig. 369)*

Fig. 369

Working

1. Take the outside right-hand end and fold it over one, under the next two. *(Fig. 370)*

2. Take the outside left-hand end and fold it over one, under two.

3. Continue the working sequence.

Fig. 370

Joining

1. The end to be joined must be on the right-hand side of the plait. Only join when there are four ends on the right. The short end must be second from the outside of the right-hand group.

2. Lay the new end over the old. *(Fig. 371)*

3. Make the right-hand move, step 3. *(Fig. 372)*

4. Leave the old end behind on the next right-hand move.

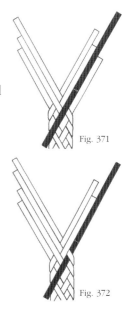

Fig. 371

Fig. 372

Finishing

1. Fasten the ends until dry. Clip off the joined ends once the finished plait is dry.

FLATTENED STRAW

Preparation

Between 1840 and 1860, in an era known as the Ornamental Period, Swiss products became even more decorative. Post horns, anchors, birds, leaves and flowers were punched from straw sheets using custom-made dies then elaborately decorated with Schnürli, narrow plaits, crystals, beads and seashells, and straw ribbons were folded into decorative motifs.

Selecting Sraw

Wheat, oats, barley and rye are all suitable. Use thick straws taken from the butt end of the top section and cut them into 20–25 cm (8–10") lengths. The second section of the plant stem, between the 1st and 2nd leaf node can be used if it will split and soften without cracking. Bleached and dyed straws provide excellent ribbons.

Dampening

Natural straw normally requires about 15 minutes soaking in hand-hot water. Bleached and dyed straws require less time; some may not need any soaking. Straws from the second section may need 60 minutes. The straws are ready when they can be bent without cracking. Drain and then wipe to remove surplus water, use immediately.

Do not leave straws soaking in water for long periods; they develop a nasty dull colour and may become too soft to use.

Splitting

Cut each end of the straw straight. Hold the straw at one end and insert the cutting tool into the hollow stem. Pull the tool along the length so that the stem cuts along one side. Use your fingers to open the stem at one end.

Put it on a firm flat work surface, pith side upwards and use the smoothing tool to open the rest of the stem.

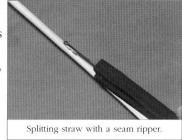
Splitting straw with a seam ripper.

Smoothing

Smooth along the pith side of the straw. Occasionally second joint straw will not soften until some but not all of the pith is scraped off. However, the rule should always be: don't remove the pith.

Work on a hard surface and stroke firmly along the length, in one direction only. Don't use a scrubbing action or you may crease or break the straw.

Smoothing straw.

Damp straw will try to revert to its tubular shape, so smooth until the straw has started to flatten, then roll up along its length, shiny side inwards and temporarily fasten with a paper clip. Put to one side until dry.

Once dry, repeat the smoothing process until the straw starts to curl like paper ribbon.

Trimming

The straw ribbon should have a constant width along its length. If the ribbon is wider at one end than the other, or if it widens in the centre, it should be trimmed to an even width using a craft knife and metal rule.

Storing

Softened straw ribbons can be stored for an indefinite period. If you want to store them flat press between sheets of card.

Before you begin

Unless otherwise stated, use dry straw sheets. Straw has a grain that affects the final appearance of the ornament. Look along the length of a straw ribbon, the appearance is shiny. Look across, the surface is dull. You can use this effect to create interesting patterns. Avoid positioning a join in the straw sheet at the edge of a motif where it will be susceptible to damage.

Straw Sheets

Making Straw Sheets

Choose a backing material that has a weight and appearance suitable for the final application of the straw sheet. If the backing will be visible then consider using a coloured backing that matches the straw colour.

You will need:

Straw ribbons
Backing paper or fabric
Non-stick paper, optional
Sticky tape
Glue and small glue brush
Smoothing tool

Damp cloth
Craft knife or scissors
Metal edge rule
Cutting board
Press

Starting

1. Stretch the backing over a firm work surface and use sticky tape to secure it to the surface. Stretch and secure open-weave fabrics to a sheet of non-stick paper or plastic that has first been taped to the surface.

Working

1. Apply a generous covering of glue to the pith side of a straw ribbon.
2. Lay the first straw ribbon on to the backing and press down.
3. Apply glue to the pith side of another straw ribbon.
4. Lay the second straw ribbon so that its long edge fits tightly against the edge of the first.
5. Press down and wipe away any surplus glue. Use a smoothing tool to carefully smooth along the length of the ribbons.
6. Continue the working sequence until the whole sheet is covered.

> **Handy hint**
> If, as the ribbons were glued to the backing, one has slightly overlapped the next, then remove the overlap by working a smoothing tool along its length.

Finishing

1. Turn over the sheet and gently smooth across the backing to expel air bubbles and straighten any creases.
2. Trim the straw ribbons to the edge of the backing.
3. Press for at least six hours in a flower press or under a heavy weight. If the straw ribbons have been glued on to open-weave backing then let the glue become tacky before putting the sheet between non-stick paper and then into the press.

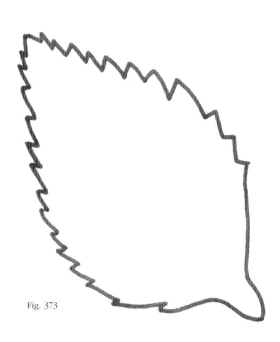

Fig. 373

Cut Ornaments

When the straw sheets are backed with paper you can use craft punches, or scissors with decorative cutting blades to cut out the ornament. Sheets backed with fabric or with fibrous paper must be cut with sharp scissors or a sharp craft knife.

Leaf with Straight Grain

Leaf ornaments of all shapes, sizes and colours were popular in the 19th century. They were either left plain or decorated with beads and thread.

You will need:

Straw sheet
Template
Sticky tape, optional
2B pencil
Craft knife or curved
blade scissors

Cutting board
Embossing tool,
ballpoint tip
Thin wire
Thin paper
Glue and glue brush

Starting

1. Copy the template, enlarging or reducing it to the required size. *(Fig. 373)*
2. Look at the straw sheet and check the direction of the grain.
3. Put the sheet on to a work surface so that the backing is uppermost.
4. Place the template, right side downwards on to the sheet so that the direction of grain runs vertically from top to bottom. *(Fig. 374)*
5. Hold or tape the template in place and use the pencil to mark around it.

Fig. 374

Working

1. Remove the template and carefully cut around the basic shape.
2. Once free of the sheet cut out the serrated edge.

> ### Handy hint
> *Sticky tape can be too sticky for attaching the template to the straw sheet; remove some of its adhesion by pressing on to a clean surface, and then apply to the straw.*

Finishing

1. The leaf can be left plain or use the ballpoint tool to mark veins on to the straw side.
2. Take a piece of fine wire the length of the leaf plus sufficient for the required stem and lay it along the central leaf vein on the back side. *(Fig. 375)*
3. Glue a piece of thin paper over the wire. Leave to dry.
4. To shape the leaf, cup your hand and lay the leaf, straw-side down into your palm. Use your fingers to gently work the leaf into your palm until it curves.

Fig. 375

Marking veins with a ballpoint tool.

Cut Ornaments

Leaf with Chevron Grain

This leaf is cut into two sections and the straw applied at an angle so that the grain creates a pattern.

You will need:

Straw sheet
Backing paper, same colour as the straw
Template
2B pencil
Craft knife or scissors

Cutting board
Glue and glue brush
Fine wire, optional
Tapestry needle
Decorative thread

Starting

1. Copy the template, enlarging or reducing it to the required size. *(Fig. 376)*
2. Check the direction of the grain on the straw sheet and if necessary mark the edge of the backing.
3. Lightly mark the back side of the template to show the direction of grain on the leaf.
4. Cut the template into two sections following the dotted line shown. *(Fig. 377)*

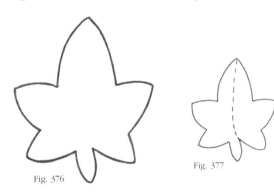

Fig. 376

Fig. 377

Use leaves as your inspiration.

Working

1. Put the straw sheet with the backing uppermost on to a firm work surface.
2. Position the two halves of the template diagonally across the grain of the straw sheet, the marked back side uppermost. *(Fig. 378)*
3. Using a pencil mark around the two halves of the template. Accuracy is important.
4. Carefully cut out the two halves.
5. Glue the two halves to the backing material.
6. Wipe off any surplus glue.

Fig. 378

Finishing

1. Trim off any excess paper from around the edge of the leaf.
2. Finish using the methods described in Leaf with Straight Grain, page 163, or stitch veins across the surface.
3. With the straw side uppermost use a sharp pointed needle to prick the holes that the thread will pass through. *(Fig. 379)*

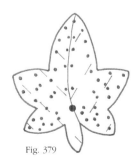

Fig. 379

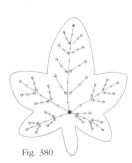

Fig. 380

Cut Ornaments

4. Use an appropriate needle for the thickness of thread and stitch the veins in the sequence shown. The central hole is the common starting point for all five main veins. *(Fig. 380)*

5. To make the long central stitch follow the curved join between the two halves, use the side stitches to hold it in place. Take the side stitch around the long stitch and through the appropriate pricked hole.

6. Secure the ends by threading them under several stitches.

7. Hide the stitches on the back by glueing over matching colour thin paper, cut to the template shape. If you want to add a wire to the leaf do so at this point, using the method described in Leaf with Straight Grain.

8. Leave to dry.

Handy hint
Use a soft thread such as cotton, linen, silk or wool. Synthetics such as polyester are more likely to tear the straw.

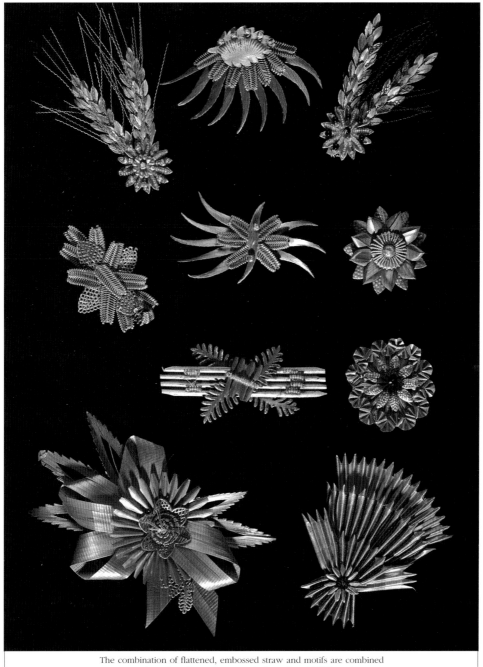

The combination of flattened, embossed straw and motifs are combined
to produce these bonnet ornaments from the mid-19th century.

Cut Ornaments

Butterfly

This ornament is decorated with beads and couched down Schnürli. Dye the Schnürli by using one of the methods provided in Appendix 1. The body is a Rat Dropping motif, see page 68.

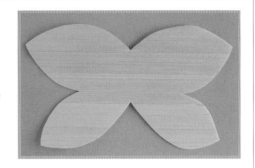

You will need:

Straw sheet
Template
2B pencil
Curved blade scissors or craft knife
Embossing tool, ballpoint tip
4 dyed Schnürli 10cm (4") long

Beads, round and oval
Rat Dropping, page 68
Decorative thread
Milliner's needle
Backing paper cut to the template shape
Glue and glue brush

Starting

1. Copy the template, enlarging or reducing it to the required size. *(Fig. 381)*
2. Place the template right side down on to the backing of the straw sheet. The straw grain must run from left to right across the wings.
3. Use the pencil to carefully mark around the template.
4. Cut out the shape using curved blade scissors.
5. Put the butterfly shape on to a firm work surface with the straw side uppermost.
6. Use a ballpoint tool to mark where the Schnürli will be stitched into place. *(Fig. 382)*

Fig. 382

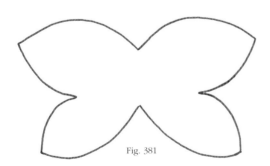

Fig. 381

Working

1. Begin by couching the first Schnürli to the top left-hand wing. The Schnürli will follow the marked line. Make a needle hole, through the straw side towards the backing, to the top right of centre.
2. Bring the threaded needle through the hole from the back to the straw side. Leave a 2.5cm (1") length of thread at the back. Temporarily hold it in place with sticky tape.
3. Dampen the first Schnürli.
4. Hold one end across the body and take the thread diagonally over the Schnürli so that the thread drops down into the ply. *(Fig. 383)*
5. Make a second hole under the Schnürli.
6. Pass the threaded needle through the hole and tighten the thread.
7. Space the stitches 3–4 mm apart.
8. At the wing tip you may need to work an extra stitch.
9. Work around the wing until you arrive back at the centre body.
10. Fasten the ends of thread on the backside by passing them under several stitches.

Fig. 383

11. Cut off the thread ends. Trim the Schnürli ends.

12. Work around the next wing using the second length of Schnürli, and then work around the two wings on the opposite side of the body.

Finishing

1. Decorate the wings with the beads, sewing them in place. Make the needle hole by pressing through from the straw side to the backing.

2. Tie off the thread ends using a double overhand knot.

3. The Rat Dropping is made by simultaneously winding three Schnürli, natural, green and pink, around a 5mm (0.25") diameter straw.

4. Use thread to stitch the Rat Dropping to the butterfly shape.

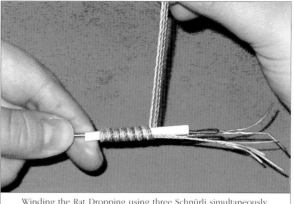

Winding the Rat Dropping using three Schnürli simultaneously.

5. Make the antennae by unwinding a Schnürli length left over when the Rat Dropping was finished.

6. Make a half-knot at the end of each antennae.

7. Trim the other ends of Schnürli.

8. Once all the decoration is applied glue the backing paper to the back of the butterfly.

> ***Handy hint***
> *Stitch across the grain to lessen the possibility of stitches tearing the straw.*

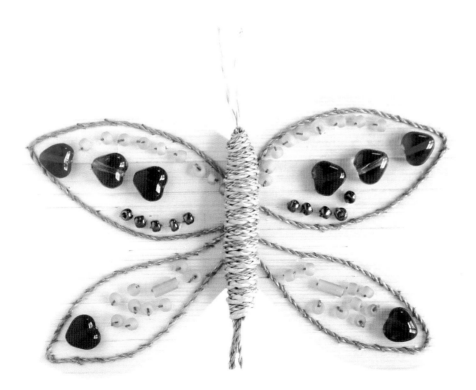

Butterfly decorated with beads.

Cut Ornaments

Pinked Circle

To provide sufficient stability this type of ornament must be cut from a straw sheet that has been backed with buckram or thick card.

You will need:

Straw sheet
Template
Pinking shears
Decorative thread
Thread

9 straw-covered beads, each 15mm diameter, page 56
3 Glass beads
Needle

Starting

1. Cut a 5cm diameter circle from the straw sheet.
2. Cut a 15mm circle from the centre of the circle.
3. Use pinking shears to cut the outer edge of the circle.
(Fig. 384)

Fig. 384

3. Thread a glass bead on to the end immediately below the lowest bead and use thread to tie in place.
4. Pass the three long ends through the centre circle.
5. Thread the three ends under the windings on the back. Secure each one by tying to an adjacent winding.

Working

1. Hold one end of the thread against the backing of the circle.
2. Wind the thread around the circle so that each winding rests in the indentation of the pinked edge.
3. Take care to keep the thread side by side as it progresses around the centre circle.
4. When the circle is covered take the end to the back.
5. Secure the end by using thread to tie it to the adjacent winding.

Finishing

1. Cut three, 10cm (4") lengths of the decorative thread.
2. Using a needle, thread three straw-covered beads on to each length.

Pinked Circle Ornament.

Cut Ornaments

Bonnet ornament.

Punched Ornaments

When using leatherwork punches, or any punch that needs hammering, put a thick heavy-duty cutting mat or the open grain end of a block of wood under the straw sheet.

Sequins (Pailletten)

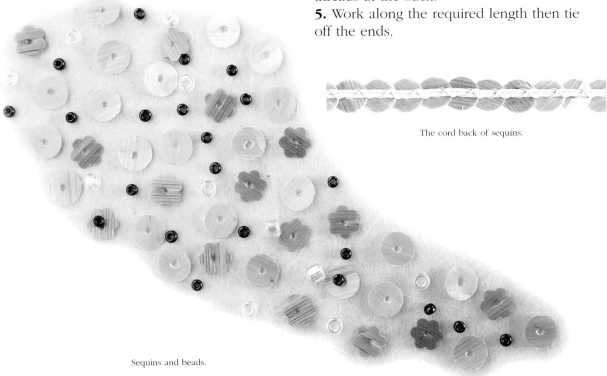

Prevent sequins from curling by using a straw sheet with a thick backing.

You will need:

Straw sheet
Round punch 6mm (0.25") diameter
Milliner's needle
Cork mat

Thread
Cord or thin cotton covered
Milliner's wire, optional

Starting

1. The shiny side of the sheet must face the cutting blade as you cut from the sheet. Always cut circles from between the joins.

Working

1. Place the circles straw side uppermost on to the cork mat.
2. Use the needle to make a hole in the centre of the sequin.

Finishing

1. Thread the sequins on to the thread. Tie a knot at the end of the thread to stop the sequins sliding off.
2. To provide additional strength, the string of sequins can be attached to a cord or thin Milliner's wire (cotton-covered wire).
3. Hold the cord or wire taut.
4. Using 2 separate threads, attach the string of sequins to the cord passing them between and under the sequins then crossing the threads at the back.
5. Work along the required length then tie off the ends.

The cord back of sequins.

Sequins and beads.

Punched Ornaments

Appliqué Sequin Ornament

The finished design has been presented as a wall hanging in the embroidery frame. It can also be worked directly onto clothing or accessories.

You will need:

Backing fabric
Fabric marker
40 sequins
Flower shape
Wicking needle

Rocaille beads, 53
crystal and 13 jet
Thread
Beading needle
Embroidery ring

Starting

1. Stretch the backing fabric over the embroidery frame and secure with the outer ring.
2. Mark the pattern on to the fabric. *(Fig. 385)*
3. Use the flower template and cut the shape from the straw sheet. *(Fig. 386)*
4. Make a hole in the centre of the flower using a wicking needle.

Working

1. Begin at the base of the pattern and first work along the left-hand line.
2. Pass the threaded needle through the fabric from the back to the front.
3. Pass it through the sequin so that its straw side is uppermost on the fabric.
4. Thread on a bead and then take the needle back through the sequin's central hole and through the fabric.
5. Add the next sequin so that it just touches the edge of the previous one.
6. Next work the centre line repeating the working sequence.
7. Finally work the right-hand line.
8. Fasten the thread ends.

Finishing

1. Attach the straw flower at the base of the sequin pattern by bringing the threaded needle from the back of the fabric and through the central hole of the motif.

2. Thread 10 beads on to the thread, alternate the colour.
3. Bring the thread up around the last bead and tie off.
4. Bring a new thread from the back of fabric, through the central hole and repeat the stringing of the beads, this time using 8. Secure in the same way as the first.
5. Make a third string of beads the same length as the second.
6. Secure the thread ends on the back of fabric.

Fig. 385

Fig. 386

Punched Ornaments

Wheat Ear

Many shapes of paper punches and scissors are now available in Craft shops. Use either an oval or teardrop shape to make this wheat ear.

You will need:

Straw sheet
Punch, oval or teardrop
8mm (0.25") long
Embossing tool,
ballpoint tip
Backing paper

Straw stem 10cm
(4") long
Fine wire 10cm (4") long
Glue and glue brush
14 Schnürli 7cm (3") long

Starting

1. Punch 28 shapes from the straw sheet making sure that there are no joins close to the edge of each one.
2. Unwind each Schnürli so that you have 28 crimped lengths.
3. Cut the backing paper into two wheat ear shapes. *(Fig. 387)*
4. Insert the wire into the straw stem.

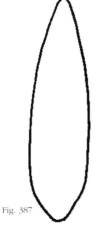

Fig. 387

Working

1. Curve each punched shape by working the backing with an embossing tool.
2. Glue an unwound Schnürli on to the back of each punched shape. Leave until dry.
3. Glue the first bearded shape to the top centre of the wheat ear template.
4. Glue the next one to the left-hand edge of the template so that it slightly overlaps the first.
5. Repeat on the right-hand side of the template, placing the shape so that it is a little lower than the one on the left.
6. Add a total of 9 bearded shapes to each side.
7. Starting at the top of the template, overlap 9 bearded shapes down the centre of the wheat ear.
8. Leave until dry.

Finishing

1. Turn the wheat ear so that the backing paper is uppermost.
2. Place the wired straw stem vertically along the length of the wheat ear.
3. Glue the second backing template over the wired stem and back of the wheat ear.
4. Trim the paper edges to the edge of the wheat ear.
5. Leave until dry.
6. Once dry, the stem can be carefully bent to the required angle.
7. Trim the beards.

These Wheat Ears are made by wiring together Mouse Dropping motifs.

Embossed Ornaments

Use straw sheets with a fibrous backing and do not over-soften the straw. Work slowly and carefully, pressing the sheet into every indentation. Embossing requires patience and some practice.

Wheat Leaf

Swiss workers used a wooden mill with serrated rollers but you can use a paper-crimping tool. The straw sheet or ribbon must be crimped whilst dry.

You will need:

> Straw sheet or ribbon
> Crimping tool
> Scissors
> Fine wire, optional
> Backing paper, optional

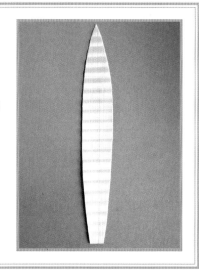

Starting

1. Cut the sheet, or trim the ribbon to an 8cm (3") long, 10mm (0.5") wide piece with the grain running along its length.

Wheat Ear and Leaf.

Working

1. Insert the end of the straw between the rollers of the crimping tool and press closed.
2. Wind the straw through the tool, keeping the edge of the straw at right angles to the rollers.

Finishing

1. Cut the straw into the shape of a gently tapering leaf.
2. Trim the base of the leaf shape so that it narrows.
3. Make a shaped leaf by glueing a wire to the straw backing, then cover with another piece of backing paper cut to the leaf shape.

> **Handy hint**
> *When glueing the crimped shapes*
> *to an additional backing use*
> *plenty of glue.*

Embossed Ornaments

Bow

Use a piece of sheet or ribbon that has a soft flexible backing and check that the straw is firmly glued to the backing.

You will need:

Straw sheet or ribbon	Thread
Crimping tool	Bead(s)
Pin	Milliner's needle
Small Rosette,	
15mm (0.5") diameter,	
page 92	

Starting

1. Cut the sheet or ribbon to a 20cm (8") long, 12mm (0.5") wide piece with the grain running along its length.
2. If the ribbon feels stiff, continue to soften it until it is very pliable.
3. On the backing make marks at 5, 10 and 15cm (2", 4" and 6").

Working

1. Crimp the straw.
2. Form the first half of the bow. Take the left-hand end and twist it across the centre point so that the 5cm mark lays on top of the centre point.
3. Form the second half. Take the right-hand end and twist it across the centre point so that the 15cm mark lays on top of the centre point.
4. Temporarily secure with a pin through the central crossover.

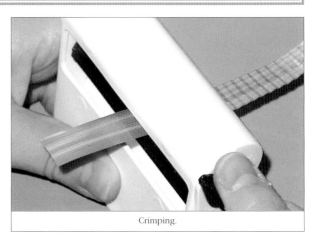

Crimping.

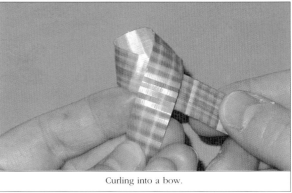

Curling into a bow.

Finishing

1. Stitch the motif to the centre of the bow.
2. Add the beads to the centre. In the example a small crystal bead sits inside a larger pearlised bead.
3. On the back of the bow tie off the thread ends.
4. Trim the ends of the bow to an angle.

Decorated bows.

Embossed Ornaments

Embossed Leaf

Choose a mould, either clay or plastic, with smooth rounded contours that are less likely to cut through the straw sheet.

You will need:
  Straw sheet with fibrous backing
  Mould
  Embossing tool(s), ballpoint tip
  Curved blade scissors
  Cutting board

Starting

1. Cut a piece of the sheet that is a little larger than the mould pattern.
2. If necessary use a tool to soften the straw sheet until it is very flexible.

Working

1. Put the sheet, straw side down, over the mould pattern.
2. Rub over the surface of the straw sheet pushing it downwards into the mould.
3. Once there are clear indentations around the edge, and high points of the mould, begin to work into the pattern. Work from the centre outward taking care not to move the straw sheet.

Decorated embossed leaf.

4. Keep working until the straw sheet is pushed into every contour of the mould. To work into all the contours you may need to use variously sized embossing tools.
5. Lift one end of the straw sheet and carefully check whether the embossing is sufficient, if it is then remove the straw sheet from the mould.

Finishing

1. Carefully cut around the edges of the shape.

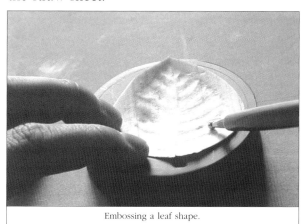

Embossing a leaf shape.

Embossed Ornaments

Stencilled Pattern

Stencils provide another method of embossing. Choose a simple design, which once embossed can be cut out from the backing sheet and decorated.

You will need:

       Straw sheet with fibrous backing
       Stencil
       Sticky tape
       Embossing tool(s), ballpoint tip
       Beads, optional

Work against a window or on a light box.

Starting

1. Tape the stencil to a light box or on to a window.
2. Put the straw sheet over the stencil, straw side against the stencil, and use tape to hold in place.

Working

1. Use the embossing tool(s) to press out the design.
2. Take time to work into every part of the stencil, paying particular attention to the stencil edges.

Finishing

1. Remove the sheet from the stencil.
2. Either cut the design from the sheet or leave the sheet intact so that the embossed pattern forms a feature on its surface.
3. The shape or pattern can be decorated with beads or with thread.

Folded Motifs

These motifs were usually made from straw ribbons without a backing. Unfortunately, no matter how careful its preparation some straw cracks along its length, so back it to a thin fibrous backing paper, preferably straw-coloured.

Thorn (Stachel)

This motif is made with the shiny side facing outward. It can be used with the arch upwards or downwards.

You will need:

> Straw ribbon 5cm (2") long, 10mm (0.5") wide
> Glue and glue brush
> Pin board, pins

Starting

1. Mark the centre point on the back side of the ribbon.
2. Dampen your fingers and carefully run them along the straw ribbon.

Working

1. Hold the straw horizontally with the shiny side down.
2. At the centre point, fold the straw at right angles to the horizontal. The end now points vertically away from you. *(Fig. 388)*
3. Make a second fold so that it lays parallel to the first. *(Fig. 389)*

Finishing

1. Overlap the ends and apply the glue to hold them in place. *(Fig. 390)*
2. Pin to the board and leave until dry.

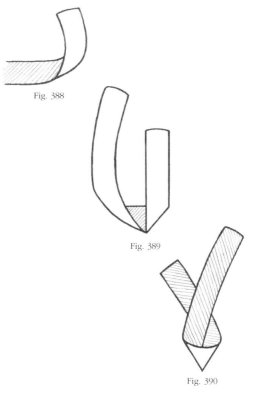

Fig. 388

Fig. 389

Fig. 390

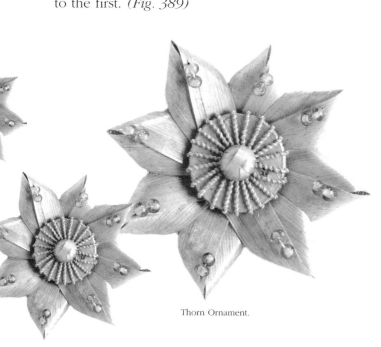

Thorn Ornament.

> **Handy hint**
> *To make matching motifs first accurately measure and cut as many pieces as you need for the finished ornament.*

Folded Motifs

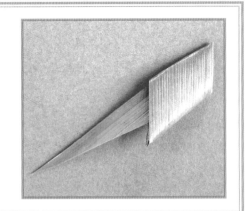

Diamond (Gefaltetes Motiv)

The width of straw ribbon will determine the finished size of motif.

You will need:

Straw ribbon 15cm (6") long, 10mm wide
Craft knife or scissors
One needle with large eye, optional

Starting

1. The ribbon must be an even width with parallel sides.
2. Cut one end of the straw so that it is at right angles to the sides.
3. Dampen your fingers and carefully run them along the straw ribbon.

Working

1. Fold the end to make a diagonal crease across the width of straw. *(Fig. 391)*
2. Fold the long end upwards and away from you. *(Fig. 392)*
3. The edge of the straw must lay alongside the edge of the previous fold. Press flat. *(Fig. 393)*
4. Unfold the first fold (made in Working step 2). *(Fig. 394)*

5. Cut along the diagonal crease to remove the triangle that was formed. *(Fig. 395)*
6. Fold the long end downwards and behind the motif. *(Fig. 396)*
7. Press flat. *(Fig. 397)*
8. Fold the long end upwards and diagonally in front of the motif. *(Fig. 398)*
9. When it is in place, press it flat. *(Fig. 399)*
10. Fold the long end downwards and behind the motif. *(Fig. 400)*
11. Press flat. *(Fig. 401)*

> **Handy hint**
> *Although not a traditional technique, you can back a dry straw ribbon with sticky tape.*

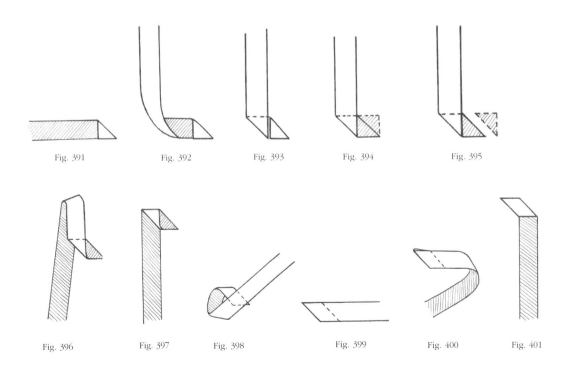

Fig. 391   Fig. 392   Fig. 393   Fig. 394   Fig. 395

Fig. 396   Fig. 397   Fig. 398   Fig. 399   Fig. 400   Fig. 401

Folded Motifs

Finishing

1. Cut the long end to a point. Shape as shown. *(Fig. 402)*

2. You can use a needle to thread the pointed end between the top and second layer of the folding. *(Fig. 403)*

3. Pull the end to tighten the motif, taking care not to spoil the shape.

Variation

Using a needle, thread one end of a Schnürli through the centre of a finished Diamond motif. Make a half-knot and then thread the second Schnürli end back through the centre. Other motifs, such as Mouse Droppings or the Small Pan Ball can also be used to decorate the end of this motif.

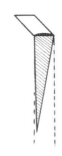

Fig. 402

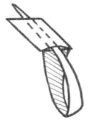

Fig. 403

Diamond variation.

Left: This hat trimming is made from Diamond motifs, Straw Beads and Chenille stitched to a concealed length of rustic plait.
Right: Prince of Wales feathers made from embossed straw and decorated with Ring plait.

Bleaching and Dyeing

BLEACHING

Bleaching is a very important process. It softens the straws making them easier to work and lightens the colour to a light primrose yellow. Bleaching and dyeing will not remove blemishes from the straws, so take care to select only clean, blemish-free stems.

 **un Bleaching**

This, the oldest known method, is normally undertaken immediately after harvest. The method is particularly suitable for rye, and can also be used to bleach grasses. To prevent shrivelling, leave the straw or grass long, cutting it below the second section and leaving the heads in place.

You will need:

Straws, heads on and cut below the second section	Weight(s) tile or large stone	**Caution**
Large container long enough to lay the straw flat	Long-handled tongs	*Boiling water*
	Protective clothing	
	Large rack(s)	

Starting

1. Make sure that the water is boiling rapidly. Turn off the heat source.
2. Carefully add the straws, laying them flat in the water.
3. Use the weight to submerge the straws.

Working

1. Leave for 10 minutes.
2. Remove the weight.
3. With great care, remove the straws and let them drain for 30 minutes.
4. Take the straws to a sunny area and spread them over a rack(s) so that air can freely circulate. They can be left in a greenhouse or conservatory.
5. The process will take several days according to the weather. The straws must be turned frequently.
6. Don't let the straws get wet or damp, this will spoil the colour.

Finishing

1. Once dry, finish preparing the straws, remove the heads and cut the straw at the first joint.
2. Store the dry straws until required.

Health and Safety Precautions

These processes involve the use of various chemicals and hot liquids. You must take extensive precautions to ensure the complete safety of yourself and others. If you are unable to follow the precautions then do not undertake these processes.

Whilst bleaching and dyeing you must:
Never carry out these processes in food preparation/eating areas.
Work in a well-ventilated area and don't inhale the fumes.
Wear protective clothing: goggles, mask, gloves and protective overalls.
Keep children, other people and animals away from the area.
Designate specific utensils and pans for bleaching and dyeing.

Protect working surfaces and the floor.
Do not use these utensils and pans for food preparation and cooking.
If using a cooker with an overhead ventilation unit make sure the unit is switched off to prevent staining of the filters.

Disposal of solutions:
Always contact your local authority to obtain advice, then follow their instructions.

Bleaching and Dyeing

This section includes two methods, one using hydrogen peroxide at room temperature and the second using gentle heating.

You must use hydrogen peroxide 60 volume (18%). Lesser strength solutions may not bleach the straw.

Bleaching with Hydrogen Peroxide (Cold)

When using cold hydrogen peroxide the bleaching process will take longer, however the benefit is that the solution can be used to bleach more than one batch of straw. To ensure even bleaching completely submerge the straws.

You will need:

Straws, without heads
Detergent
Container, strong plastic or
stainless steel (a fish kettle
is ideal)

Protective clothing
Hydrogen peroxide 60
volume (18%)
Weight
Long-handled tongs

> **Caution**
>
> *Protect your eyes.*
> *Do not inhale*
> *the fumes.*

Starting

1. Wash the straws in hand-hot water with added detergent. Rinse thoroughly and drain.
2. Carefully pour the hydrogen peroxide into the container.
3. Add the straws and add the weight. The straws must be submerged.

Working

1. To achieve the palest colour you may need to leave the straws in the solution overnight.
2. Carefully remove the straws from the container, rinse thoroughly in warm water, drain and dry.
3. The hydrogen peroxide can be reused until it no longer bleaches the straws.

Finishing

1. Dry the straws and store until required.
2. Once the bleaching action stops, the peroxide has been neutralised and can be disposed of using a method recommended by your local authority.

Bleaching and Dyeing

Bleaching with Hydrogen Peroxide (Warm)

By gently heating the hydrogen peroxide the bleaching time is reduced. The solution must not exceed simmering point; otherwise it will degenerate before bleaching occurs.

You will need:

Straws, without heads
Detergent
Stainless steel container, such as a fish kettle

Protective clothing
Hydrogen peroxide
Thermometer
Long-handled tongs

Caution
Work in a well-ventilated area.

Starting

1. Follow the previous instructions.

Working

1. Heat the hydrogen peroxide to 67°C (135°F). This temperature is below simmering point.
2. Depending upon their quantity and original colour, the straws will bleach in 30 minutes or less.
3. Carefully remove the straws. Rinse thoroughly, drain and dry.

Finishing

1. Follow the previous instructions.

Bleaching and Dyeing

DYEING

In this section there are three methods for dyeing straws. Natural straws can be dyed with great success. To achieve strong colours dye bleached straws.

NATURAL DYES

The earliest dyes came from natural substances such as madder, cochineal, indigo, fustic and logwood. Although by comparison with modern dyes these will produce a relatively limited colour range, the colours are strong and stable, provided they are not exposed to strong sunlight for long periods. Since there are so many possibilities, find a book on natural dyes. Select the materials that are suitable for dyeing plant fibres, such as onion skins, tea, blackberries and turmeric. To achieve variations in colour use the suggested mordents.

Food Colourings

Although these may not always be as lightfast as some other dyes, they will produce both strong colours and wonderful shades. For paler colours, dilute the food colouring with water.

You will need:

Straws cut to the length of the bottle
Plastic bottle with tight fitting lid
Protective clothing
Liquid food colouring

Caution

Food colouring stains.

Starting

1. The bottle must be large enough to hold the straws.
2. Carefully pour the food colouring into the bottle. Use approximately 38ml of food colouring in a 1 litre bottle.
3. Add the straws.
4. Secure the bottle cap.

Working

1. Shake the bottle so that the straws are covered in the colouring.
2. Shake at regular intervals.
3. Remove the straws once the required colour is achieved. This may take five minutes; it could take a few days.

Finishing

1. Remove the straws, rinse thoroughly in warm water, drain and dry.
2. The dry straws can be stored until required.

Bleaching and Dyeing

COMMERCIAL DYES

Choose dyes that are designed for cotton, linen and other plant fibres. Hot water dyes are most successful. Cold water dyes which take longer to act, are best used on bleached straws, and only reliably produce certain colours (orange, yellow, green and brown).

The instructions included in the dye pack may advise you to add salt to the solution. It acts as a fixative when dyeing fabrics. It can also increase the resistance to fading but is normally unnecessary when dyeing straws.

The final colour effect will vary according to the chemical content of the water used. Hard water can inhibit the uptake of the dye. To counteract this problem add a commercial water softener (Sodium Sesquicarbonate or similar) to the water, follow the manufacturer's recommended dosage. Alternatively, use soft or distilled water.

When dyeing natural straws it is difficult to achieve red and blue. Natural straw is yellow so when mixed with a red dye the final colour has orange tones. Blue dyes produce green tones. To avoid this problem dye, bleached straws.

Commercial Dyeing

You will need:

Straws cut to the length	Weight
of the container	Long-handled tongs
Detergent	Protective clothing
Stainless steel container,	Hot water dye
such as a fish kettle	
with lid	

> **Caution**
> *Work in a well-ventilated area.*

Starting

1. Wash the straw in hot water with detergent. Rinse thoroughly and drain.

2. If you are using a water softener, dissolve it in the water before the dye is added.

3. Make up the dye solution, you will need to experiment with the proportion of dye to water.

Working

1. Once the dye has dissolved, add the straws, they must be submerged.

2. Bring the water to simmering point 85°C (185°F). Don't boil the solution; it is wasteful and doesn't improve the final effect. Cover the pan.

3. Check the straw colour after 10 minutes, and then at regular intervals until the required colour is achieved.

4. You can achieve various shades by using the same solution for more than one batch of straw.

5. Carefully remove the straws from the container. You can let the solution cool first.

6. Rinse thoroughly, drain and dry.

Finishing

1. Store the dry straws until required.

2. The dye solution must be used within two days.

3. Dispose of the solution as recommended by the local authority.

4. Before use, wipe the straws with a soft dry cloth to remove loose dye and to polish the surface.

> ***Handy hint***
> *If you want to repeat a specific colour then remember to make a note of the strength of solution.*

Tools and Templates

Swiss workers often made their own tools, but they took time and care to make each one sturdy and reliable. They knew that an inefficient tool causes the user endless problems. Do follow their example. In this appendix all tool templates are reproduced at actual size.

SPLIT STRAW

Needle Holder

Take a block of wood, 8cm long x 4cm wide x 15mm thick (3.125" x 1.6" x 0.5"), and into one end drill five holes, spaced 5mm (0.2") apart. The holes must be of a size which will firmly hold the needles parallel to each other. The holder must fit comfortably in your hand, so you may need to adjust its size. Smooth any sharp edges.

Tensioning block

Take a piece of wood, approximately 9cm square, 3cm thick (3.5" x 3.5" x 1.25") and hammer in three nails as shown in the template. In the place of nails you can insert three pieces of dowel into the block.

Wire holder

Take an empty plastic photographic film container and make a hole in the side. Thread the end of the wire through the hole and then put the spool of wire inside. Replace the cap. Make a wire grip: wind an elastic band around the outside of the container and pass the wire under it.

Little Star tool (Sternli)

Take a 5cm square, 2cm thick (2" x 2" x 0.75") piece of wood, and in the centre mark a circle 2cm (0.75") diameter. Make six equally spaced marks around the circumference of the circle, as shown (12, 2, 4, 6, 8 and 10 o'clock). At each mark drill a hole that is a slightly smaller diameter than the diameter of each pin. Take six long panel pins and file each point to a blunt end. Push the panel pins through from the underside to the top, it may be necessary to glue each one in place. Take a piece of card or plastic and make six holes, to match the position of the pins. Drop the card over the pins, it should lift off easily. The card will enable easy removal of the finished motif.

Tensioning block.

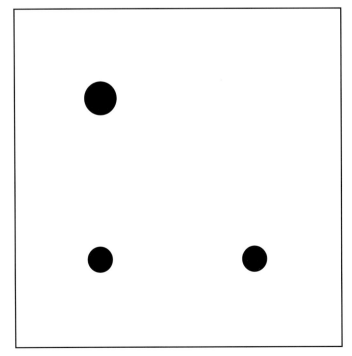

Little Star tool.

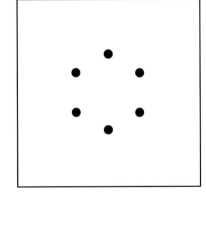

Tools and Templates

STRAW THREAD

Wheel Plait wheel (Rädligeflecht-rädli)

Make an improvised tool by inserting pins into knotting blocks. They must be fixed at a backward angle. Make two rows of pins spaced between 3cm and 7.5cm apart (1.25"–3"). The distance between each pin must be 5mm (<0.25"). The pins can be set as two straight lines, or with the left-hand line straight and the right-hand as a scallop or zig-zag, or with both edges shaped.

Square Rosette tool

Take a piece of wood, 15cm long x 20mm wide x 6mm thick (6" x 0.75" x 0.25"). Measure 45mm (1.75") from one end and put the template over the wood. The lowest pin must be at the 45mm mark. The top pin will be approximately 5mm from the opposite end. Using the method for making a Sternli tool, insert the pins, so that the right-hand row of pins is 3mm from the right-hand edge of the wooden block. Make a needle holder. On the back left-hand side cut out sufficient recess to let in the template board, so that it is flush with the left-hand edge and with the back of the holder. Glue and screw, or glue and pin the board to the holder. Drill two holes, for holding the needles, into the end of the holder. The first must be 5mm from the right-hand edge of the board, the second 5mm to the right of the first. Use two, 14cm (5.5") long needles in this tool.

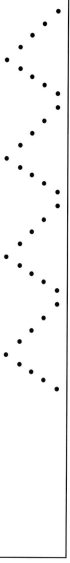

Square Rosette tool.

Tools and Templates

WHOLE STRAW

Leaf boards

Use each template as a pattern for inserting panel pins into a wooden block, individual sizes are given below. Follow the method for making a Sternli tool.

Schnürli Ear (Schnürli-ähre)

Drawing 1
Wooden board size: 9cm long x 6.5cm wide x 1cm thick (3.5" x 2.375" x 0.375")

Wheat Ear (Halmenähre)

Drawing 2
Wooden board size: 9cm long x 6.5cm wide x 1cm thick (3.5" x 2.375" x 0.375")

Leaf with Outline – various shapes

Drawing 3
Wooden board size: 13.5cm long x 7.5cm wide x 1cm thick (5.25" x 3" x 0.375")
Drawing 4 and *Drawing 5*
Wooden board size: 10cm long x 7.5cm wide x 1cm thick (4" x 3" x 0.375")

Trefoil Leaf

Drawing 6
Wooden board size: 11.5cm long x 11.5cm wide x 1cm thick (4.5" x 4.5" x 0.375")

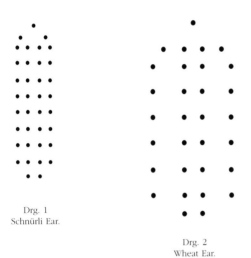

Drg. 1
Schnürli Ear.

Drg. 2
Wheat Ear.

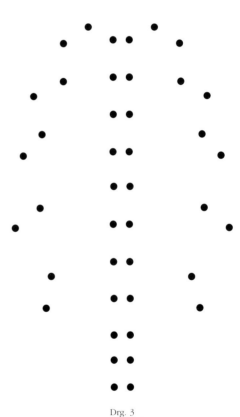

Drg. 3
Leaf with Outline.

Tools and Templates

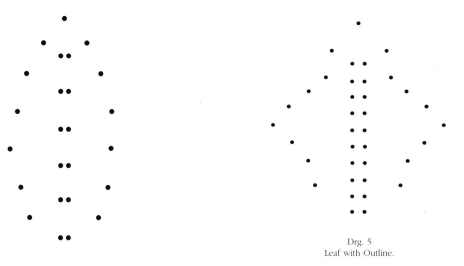

Drg. 4
Leaf with Outline.

Drg. 5
Leaf with Outline.

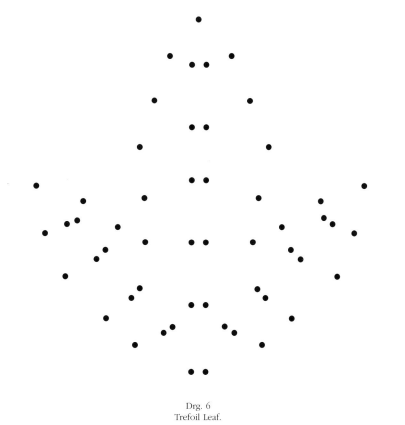

Drg. 6
Trefoil Leaf.

GENERAL INFORMATION

CONTRIBUTORS

Rita Boschung-Bielmann, Margaret Bradbury, Monika Brügger, Janet Christenot, Liselotte Helfer-Rupp, Brigitte Kilchmann, Brigitte Koch-Berger, Linda Meeker, Atie Nijenhuis-Britting, Gillian Nott, Peter Shelley, Ursula Späni-Küng, Marian Vavra, Denise Watts.
Angel on page 48 developed from an original idea by Joan Dulcey, Maryland, U.S.A.

IMAGE CREDITS

All images by Veronica Main with the exception of the following.
Cover, title page, back cover photograph and those on pages 6, 8, 9, 13, 17, 117, 165 reproduced with the kind permission of the Board of Directors of the Freiämter Stroh Museum, Wohlen. Some first appeared in *Strohzeiten* published by AT Verlag.
Photographs on pages 16, 19, 51 reproduced with the kind permission of Luton Museum Service.
Image on page 25 by Hubert Boschung, page 23 (Thistle) by Antony Gay, page 141 by Walter Kilchmann.
Map illustration on page 7 by Roger Courthold.

SELECTED BIBLIOGRAPHY

Strohzeiten, Isler, Kuhn, Wohler, Hohl, Littmann, AT Vertlag, 1991.
Von der alten Freiämter Stroh-Handflechterei zur modernen Hutgeflechtindustrie, G. Rodel, 1960.
Georges Meyer & Co. Ltd. Souvenir Book.
Die Strohindustrie im aargauischen und luzernischen Seetal, G. Rodel, 1950.
Die Technik in der Freiämter, Seetaler und Obwalder Strohflechterei, G. Rodel, 1949.
M. Bruggisser & Co. Wohlen Centenary, 1912.
Die Aargauische Strohindustrie, Hans Lehman, 1896.

SUPPLIERS

Since the current suppliers of materials and equipment will change over a period of time, contact one of the many Straw Work Associations, details given below. They will provide up to date information. Suppliers and information can also be found by searching the Internet.

STRAW WORK ASSOCIATIONS

Great Britain
Guild of Straw Craftsmen *, Crafts Council, 44a Pentonville Road, Islington, London N1 9BY.
www.strawcraftsmen.co.uk
* The Crafts Council will provide a current contact address.

Switzerland
Freiämter Stroh Museum, Bankweg 1/Kirchplatz, 5610 Wohlen.

Schweizerische Stiftung Strohverarbeitung, Cité-Bellavue 6, Postfach 151, 1707 Freiburg.
www.strohverarbeitung.ch/

U.S.A
National Association of Wheat Weavers **
PO Box 344, 11208 E. 82nd Avenue, Buhler, Kansas 67522.
www.geocities.com/Heartland/Plains/4565/naww.htm
** NAWW will supply details of other Associations within individual States.

Contact Address:
Main Collins Publishing
PO Box 926
High Wycombe
Bucks. HP15 7ZQ
Tel/Fax: 01494 714141

INDEX

Page numbers in *italics* indicate that information is given only in an illustration.